Everything
SUCKS

For everyone who is sure they will never fit in.
And for my parents,
who taught me that it's just more fun not to.

CONTENTS

chapter one

FAMILY SUCKS

I am the firstborn human.

A smear of phosphorescent firefly guts illuminates my left cheek like cosmic war paint.

"Amelia!" I scold. "You're supposed to put them in the jar, not squish out their insides!" Seven-year-old me is furious. I hate her.

My mother laughs as Amelia snatches up another bug, squeezes, then sucks out a juicy droplet of glowing goo with gusto. A neon trail dribbles down her chin.

"Eeeiw! Ma, I *told* you she doesn't know how to play."

"She's just trying to be helpful, Hannah," my mother assures me.

"Well, she's not!" I shout, grabbing the jar and stomping over to the other side of the yard to avoid anymore unwanted monkey interferences.

You see, I am the firstborn human, but Amelia is the firstborn.

If Amelia would just stick to the rules of firefly-catching, she'd make an excellent teammate. Her reflexes are undeniably swift, and she can see so well in the dark that she doesn't even need to wait for a bug to glow to spot it. But she never, ever listens—not to me or to my mother or even to the huge Great Dane down the street. As far as I can tell, monkeys in suburbia can do whatever they damn well please.

No matter how many cute shenanigans I pull, I am forever outshined by a family member who garners wild applause simply by serving herself spaghetti with her own foot. And that's not even the half of it. My parents have to call my kindergarten teacher to explain that a monkey really *did* tear up my homework collage. Nobody wants to have play dates with *me*, but even the most popular older girl in my elementary school clamors for an invitation to visit when she discovers that I am "That Monkey Girl." Living in the shadow of a one-foot-tall simian sensation totally sucks. On the bright side, I've become extremely adept at picking things up with my toes.

You're probably wondering where she came from. We all are, actually. The truth is that nobody expected her to live this long. She was born somewhere in South America, kidnapped by poachers, then sold to merchants in Egypt who ripped out her teeth. We think they taught her to pickpocket distracted tourists in town squares because she is a remarkably good thief. She's a sly magpie with an opposable thumb. She was in opium withdrawal when she was confiscated in a California customs office. She was also about to die.

My mother was working at the time for a program that trained monkeys to assist quadriplegics. My father was on a music tour and happily agreed to let my mother house the ailing primate for a few weeks before her eventual demise.

That was twenty-nine years ago.

It would be difficult to find two people more opposite than my parents in absolutely every way. My mother is perfectly proportioned and olive-skinned and is always telling me to turn off the lights and wear a jacket and remember that wearing a scarf in the car with the window open is an "invitation for decapitation." Dad takes a rounder approach to most everything, explaining that sometimes the very best ideas come from whistling, that there's never just one solution to a problem, and that everything is better with lemon meringue pie.

Long ago, death and divorce solidified Mom's foundational fear that always, at any given moment, something absolutely freaking awful is about to happen. Seriously, watch out. There's a ninety percent chance that whatever you're doing right now could result in a horrific, crippling accident. Paper cuts can lead to gangrene, cancer will find you no matter what you eat, and you have certainly been kidnapped by psychotic terrorist cannibals before she ever assumes you might be stuck in traffic.

Dad, on the other hand, thinks "Psychotic Terrorist Cannibals" sounds like a great title for a musical. And maybe he'll write, direct, and star in a full-scale production of said musical, and build six-foot-tall, dancing puppets to be his co-stars. From the time that I am old enough to support the Giant Tap Dancing Teeth Costume, I spend each holiday season performing in Dad's annual Kids' Silly Song Sing-Along Tour, kick-ball-changing my way through the humiliation-stravaganza that is running into your current elementary school crush while dressed as a set of giant, gleaming white teeth. Not even a *cool* person looks cool rubbing against a toothbrush the size of a car. So. Clearly, I don't stand a chance.

Another child of divorce, Dad moved out at fifteen. He had a hit record by twenty-two. Over that sunny New York City summer, his mutt, Barker, befriended a neurotic Doberman Pinscher named Jesse, who happened to belong to the prettiest, saddest girl in the whole wide world, aka my mother. They fell in love. First the dogs, then the owners. Just like in the movies.

My mother is quick to remind me that just because she met my father in the park doesn't mean that the park is not "a major recipe for rape," and that I shouldn't trust guys just because they have nice dogs or handsome smiles or broken arms, because that's how Ted Bundy lured women into his van of death.

"What?!"

"It's true, Hannah."

"Ma, what does that have to do with dropping me off at the library?"

"Dogs, broken arms, candy . . . predators lurk at the library. I don't want you to—"

"Boy, I sure do love dogs," Dad exclaims, apparently not listening at all, which is about as surprising as the fact that Friday follows Thursday. "Barker's the reason that you're around, you know," Dad tells me for the thousandth time. "If he hadn't been so persistent, I don't think your mother would have ever given me the time of day."

"He was a very handsome dog," she adds.

"And he taught me so much about enjoying life!" Dad muses. The napkin he is fiddling with begins to take the shape of a crumply, four-legged creature. "When I really *listened* to what Barker wanted to do, I found myself exploring new places, exercising, socializing, and just appreciating the little things. Sunshine . . . blankets . . . hot dogs!" Dad smiles, enjoying the memory.

Mom says she doesn't remember anything between the ages of nine and twelve, starting with the night her older sister Dianne stopped complaining about the headache that had been bothering her all day after she bonked her head on the side of the pool. Dianne stopped complaining because Dianne was dead.

I'm pretty sure Dad's father isn't dead, but I don't know what he looks like. Dad remembers the day he left. Dad remembers everything between the ages of nine and twelve. He even has songs about it. He closes his eyes when he sings the line, "Daddy, I wish to God I knew, how come I try so hard to be not like you?"

My dad rents out the local baseball field for one evening every year and invites people from town—the accountant, the piano teacher, the guy from the deli whose cute twin boys are in my class—and he pitches slow and easy and doesn't keep score. He keeps me at bat even after I swing and miss three times, then four times. He smiles and throws slower, easier. Underhand. "You can do it, sweetie!" Everyone is watching. Five times. Six times. "One more time!" Seven. I miss. Eight. He smiles. "Lucky number nine!" *Crack.* Finally!

But it's a foul ball. Back to the plate. I think I hate him, and then I hate myself for thinking so.

My mother is beautiful. We look completely different. Some-

times when she comes to school for parent-teacher confer-
ences, the teachers want to know if I am in touch with my
birth mother.

"What the hell are you talking about? I am her birth
mother."

Mom says I'm not to curse on playdates or at school or in
museums, but that she doesn't care what the hell I say in the
house because words aren't dangerous, like matches or the
radiation you'll absorb if you watch chicken nuggets cooking
in the microwave.

I'm doing my fifth-grade history project on the kitchen table
and my mother is bandaging up Amelia's foot.

"This is a lot of pus," Mom says to herself. "Dean, wanna see?"

She squeezes the abscess and the monkey screams. My
dad lifts his head slowly, processing the request as though
he's listening to soft banjo music echoing through clouds.

"What in the world makes you think that I would want to
see that?" he replies, returning to his paper.

"It's green. And it's still draining. Last chance."

"I think I can handle missing out on this one."

"Suit yourself." She gives it one last squeeze and wipes off
the oozing pus with the tablecloth. *Eiw.* "The transmission
stalled again today."

"I'll take a look at it."

"Take it to the mechanic," she tells him in a sharp tone. "I
need a working car. I can't take the kids to school via *shoe.*"

Dad's eyes grow large. He gets up and begins to pace, rubbing his belly and puffing out his cheeks, deep in thought. He
spears a bagel from the breadbox with his finger and spins it

carefully, studying. "It's brilliant," he declares secretively, then disappears downstairs. Twenty minutes later he emerges clutching a piece of paper with blue scribbles all over it. "We are building a Shoe Car," he announces matter-of-factly.

"A what?"

"A Shoe Car! Perfect in form and function." He points to the crude outline of a tennis shoe with giant circles sticking out from the sides. "Look at the slopes! It's so . . . aerodynamic! And with a lightweight canvas outer shell, it'll be swift enough to—"

"Trans-*mission*," Mom interrupts. "And look at the gutters!" She points to the window, through which a sloping piece of detached gutter dangles precariously.

"Are you even listening? Look at the steering mechanism! Isn't it *ingenious*?"

"We need new gutters before winter. Nobody needs a shoe car. Ever."

Dad is completely nonplussed. "Kids?"

My little brother Sam and I look at each other uncomfortably. There's really no good answer. If you take Dad's side, Mom becomes even more naggingly critical than usual, but if you don't support him, he's heartbroken. Then you remember the time he drove two hours through three feet of snow to pick you up from a sleepover when you had a tummyache, or the time he spent the entire weekend helping you craft a four-tiered Styrofoam cake hat that won the third-grade Hat Day competition, and you feel like an ungrateful brat. I know from experience that the gutters are never going to be fixed and that my mother will find some excuse to be miserable no matter what, so I side with Dad.

"Sounds great," Sam agrees.

Mom says nothing, only bites her lip, tugging on her right earlobe. She positions the monkey on her lap in prime booger-picking position. She's annoyed. "Mmm, got a big one . . ." she mutters to herself, extracting a pebble-sized ball of brown mucus. I think my mom likes animals because they can't disappoint her.

We build a Shoe Car. It is six feet long and painted blue and Dad even manages to convince Mom to hand-sew thirty-foot-long shoelaces. He has to get out and push it up the steep hills, but that doesn't stop him from showing it off, proud as can be, all over town. I'm proud of the sunny yellow bumpers and the big cartoon eyelets I helped craft out of plastic Fisher-Price rings, and proud of my dad for being so creative. I am sure that arriving at school in the amazing giant blue shoe that I helped build will finally erase my monkey moniker once and for all. Hannah the Amazing. Hannah the Magnificent!

Genevieve, the coolest, most popular girl in my elementary school, who even wears a real bra, takes one look at me pulling up in the Shoe Car and howls with laughter. Here is some excellent advice: if you don't want your new nickname to be the same as your old one except with a big fat "freak" added to the end of it, as in "That Monkey-Girl *Freak*," then the Shoe Car debut is not a winning strategy.

"You people are ruthless!" Mom shouts out my brother's window. "We don't have anything for you to take!" She storms down the stairs and throws open the front door to show the men in black suits the busted TV set, the doors that don't close, and the elaborate system of tiered trash bags tacked to the basement ceiling in case the pipes burst. Again. The men take a few notes, look a little puzzled, and then leave. Dad says that they think he might be laundering money. I don't know exactly what that means, but I'm quite sure by looking around the house that nothing of any sort is being laundered here.

Other dads put on ties every morning to go to work, but my dad is rarely up before noon and rarely clad in anything more than Tighty-Whities. It's gross. Not as gross as the dead cat in the freezer, but still.

Sometimes people in the neighborhood bring their pets to Mom in an emergency. If the pet is in too much pain and doesn't have a chance, she'll euthanize it and store it in the freezer behind the peas and carrots until the owners can figure out what to do with it. We don't remember who owned that frozen cat. Every now and then when I'm rooting around for a frozen pizza, I'll accidentally grab a handful of tail through the plastic bag like I'm in some really bad horror movie.

Hollywood said Amelia was too ugly to be the close-up monkey in the horror movie that she starred in, but she still got to do all the stunts, like lighting people on fire and injecting them with poison. Amelia bought our house with her salary from the movie. Dad doesn't like to talk about that.

Once, when Sam was a baby, Amelia tried to toss a hair dryer into the bathtub, a stunt for which she had been rewarded with many mini marshmallows on the movie set. Even though the hair dryer wasn't plugged in, I still got in trouble. Amelia didn't.

Sometimes I feel like my mother is looking through a window at the alternate-dimension life she would have had if Dad had become the rock star everybody thought he would. He was on the fast track until a combination of bad luck and worse management landed him on the music industry blacklist. In another life, my mother would fly first class and eat out at fancy restaurants and wouldn't have to remind Dad to put on a nice jacket. Or maybe he'd be such a rock star that he *could* wear dirty T-shirts to fancy restaurants, because he's freakin' DEAN FRIEDMAN, and he could *buy* this restaurant if he wanted to, so he can do whatever he wants. Actually, he *does* do whatever he wants, which kind of confuses me. But it seems like if you're wealthy, you don't have to explain yourself. You have an excuse. You're just that eccentric billionaire.

Dad sometimes designs interactive museum instruments like harps with lasers for strings or volcanic fiberglass sculptures covered in orange bicycle horns arranged in spiraling chromatic scales. But even the virtual reality video games, the time-travel TV show, and the talking guitar never managed to take off and shower my mother with all the money and security she imagined she was destined for at twenty-two. Perhaps because of this disappointment, she is rarely supportive of his ideas.

Which is why I am absolutely horrified to discover that Mom is now on board with Dad's latest plan to yank me out of sixth grade and move the entire family onto a tour bus all the way across the Atlantic Ocean in order to promote his new album. It's a big deal, his first partnership with the record industry in seventeen years. Even so, I am *not* missing the first year of middle school to rove around the English countryside, sharing a bed with my smelly little brother in a smelly little bus. I'm not going.

Amelia is draped over Mom's shoulder. They both stare me

down intensely.

"We have fed you and clothed you and paid for piano lessons and glitter rainbow shoes, and I spent sixteen hours in labor with you, and now we've finally found a competent monkey-sitter after *twenty-seven* interviews, so you. Are. *Going.*"

And I go.

chapter two

PERIODS SUCK

Sometimes the road is a magical place. We travel to ancient castles where the wind whips across the green Irish hillside with such force that you can lean all the way into it without falling over. We see double rainbows and gamble at racetracks and ride in long skinny boats with gardens on the roof that sail down English canals in neat little rows. We visit chocolate factories and play music in haunted theaters and eat Twinkies for dinner at three in the morning. Everyone says Dad's album is going to be a huge hit. We're finally going to be rich and Mom will never complain and Dad's going to play to sold-out concert halls full of screaming fans, just like when he started out. The album poster even appears on big red double-decker buses all around London. We're famous.

The best part is that I don't have to go to school. Every week or so, Mom asks Sam and me what we want to learn about and we make a plan. For architecture, we visit palaces and cathedrals and I build a scale model of the Tower of London. For theater, we see shows on the West End and take walking tours of the Royal Opera House and stand on the steps of Saint Paul's, where Eliza Doolittle would have sold Henry Higgins that fateful flower. I want to learn about fashion, so we visit the Victoria and Albert Museum to study four centuries of European clothing—corsets, crinoline, gorgeous hoopskirts. There's even a whole exhibit on tiaras. I am in heaven.

When the tour seems to be doing well, Dad hires four cheap twenty-something musicians—a pixie-haired saxophonist, a tattooed bassist, a manic drummer, and a beer-guzzling guitarist whose name I never catch— to be his band, and they move onto the bus with us. I try to be cool in front of them, but it's hard to be a rebel when you are confined to a bus the size of a bathroom with your entire family. My only means of financial independence comes from the pittance I am paid for managing Dad's mailing list database, and I need to cooperate to have enough pocket money to spend on quirky items from all the strange places we visit. I learn to juggle an hourglass-shaped Chinese yo-yo at an international festival and how to sew patched jeans under a colorful tent at an Irish crafts fair. I am enthralled by the bustling bohemian markets of Camden—ancient cobblestones and neon green Mohawks; winding alleyways filled with exotic tapestries, sparkly fishnet stockings, and Buddha figurines hand-carved from walnuts; old men in weather-beaten stalls hawking fresh fish and chips with pickles and peas and truffles filled with cognac and cappuccino crème.

I buy flowing harem pants with sequins from a shop that smells of warm red spices. The saxophonist picks up a sachet of henna from the adjoining stall, and she shows me how to draw temporary tattoos on my hands. Sax and I mix the pigment and then squeeze wormy little lines of henna from the tip of a plastic bag into swirls and paisley peacocks and feathery earthen rings. We listen to Louis Armstrong and wait for the clay to dry until it cracks and feels tight and pulls at our skin, and then we scratch it off to reveal dark tan patterns that map our giggles through long six-hour rides of countryside boredom as we drive from town to town.

But soon I start to feel claustrophobic. Sleeping inside a cramped, itchy vehicle that smells like wet dog behind a drummer who compulsively tap-a-tap-taps at all hours of the day, even if the only remotely percussive object in reach is a breadstick, and sharing a bed with your spastic little brother and an oversized bass case while your parents have intense discussions about "finances" and "responsibility" in gritted whispers, as if the entire damn bus can't hear everything they say, is pretty much as far from magical as you can get. The only time I encounter people my own age is when I am forced to hock CDs featuring a picture of my parents making out on the cover to *their* parents, who have dragged them to the concert against their will and smoosh CDs in their faces, saying, "Oooh, darling, did you know that you were *conceived* to this song?" Dad won't stop making bad puns. Mom won't stop complaining. British people use weird words and eat pizza with a knife and fork and I don't have any friends here and I want to go home.

I express my indignation with a lot of arm-folding and eye-rolling and many self-imposed silence-strikes, which usually do not have the effect I intend.

"I'm going to pick up some chocolate ice cream after the show for anybody who *says* they're interested . . . " Dad tempts.

My brother is less tactful in his attempts to engage me. "I'm calling you snotbuttface from now on. That's okay, right, snotbuttface? OW! Snotbuttface *pinched* me!"

Even in spite of my frequent silence-strikes, our ancient Scottish driver and road manager, Gabhran, is still the quietest member of the tour. I'm convinced he's actually a mute for three months until a petrol station in Aberdeen is all out of cigarettes and he mutters something quickly with a lot of "feck" and "shite" in a creaky Scottish brogue. He survives, as far as I can tell, on cigarettes, black coffee, and hard rock alone. He does not smile. He does not eat. He never takes off his sunglasses, and he has a full beard the likes of which I've only seen on TV wizards and ZZ Top. The combination makes it impossible to tell whether he's annoyed, asleep, or even freakin' alive. He was a professional racecar driver until he broke thirty-nine bones in an accident and became a road manager for traveling bands. My mother is not impressed when Dad tells her the story.

"Why don't we just throw the kids out the window now and save them the trouble?"

"Honey, everybody loves this guy. He does headliners, international tours—he's the best!"

Mom heaves the final box of CDs in the back of the bus and slams the trunk with intention. "Then why the hell is he with us?"

After a while I stop kneeling in the catwalks to watch my dad perform. He is amazing, engaging, his performance virtuosic, but I can't stand peering down at half- and then quarter-full audiences. The advertising budgets have been slashed, Dad's manager stops returning his calls, and pretty soon we're opening to twelve people in a twelve-hundred-seat theater. We're losing money. Even the local radio shows cancel on us. I feel like I'm letting the family down when CD sales drop so low they don't even cover the cost of gas. I try new pitches. I make flashier signs and start accosting people in the lobby during intermission to guilt them into buying the stacks of unsold merchandise. "Pay for my college education!" I tell them, which seems to make people laugh, though I know it's hardly a joke.

My mother is livid. The tour is a bust.

"I left my animals. I left everything for this—this—this idiotic fantasy!"

"You're the one who said we owed it to ourselves to give it one last—do you *know* what we could have had if we hadn't decided to keep—"

"Shutupshutupshutup!" I finally shout after 65 kilometers of pretending to ignore the passive-aggressive whispers. "You're *both* wrong!"

Mom explains she's not upset, that this just wasn't what she expected. Dad explains he's not upset either, that nothing is wrong and this is all part of the plan and everyone should try to just enjoy the ride. I explain that I am *majorly* upset. I haven't taken a proper shower in weeks and I'm missing the first big middle school dance on Friday and nobody ever asked me if I wanted to do this in the first place. They tell me to stop being so overdramatic.

I never thought I'd miss being That Monkey Girl who gets good grades, but now that the only person to hang out with is my little brother and nobody gives me gold stars even when I do a really good job, I realize with a twinge of terror that spending another year like this on the road is going to turn me into something much worse than a girl with a strange pet. I'll become a crazy social recluse just like my parents. I'll become my mother, unwittingly insulting hostesses by telling them that the viscosity of their fancy hollandaise sauce reminds me of phlegm. I'll become my father, breaking world records for wallpaper-staring while the party of the century unfolds around me. In order to forestall this awful fate, I resolve to actively chat with roadies and venue managers, to befriend stage hands, to make everybody laugh, if only to keep the monotony of six-hour road trips from driving me slowly insane. The monotony of six-hour road trips halts the night that we almost die.

The night that we almost die also happens to be the night of the big dance back home. I am awakened from a dream in which I am slow-dancing with Nick Nunzio, the most popular boy in school, by the sound of gunfire and blaring horns as the bus starts to convulse like the universe is in a giant blender—*Krrkrrrrkkrrrrr!*—am I still dreaming? Someone screams. Everything flips sideways. Instruments and sheet music and boxes of CDs tumble out from overhead racks, raining down all over as a low, metallic growl fills the bus. And then, everything is suddenly still—silent, except for the wispy *ssshooms* of cars on the highway speeding past.

According to the road crew, if it hadn't been for Gabhran's deft and lightning-fast maneuvering after the tire exploded as we charged down the highway, we would have careened straight into oncoming traffic and been pummeled to a pulp.

"It's jes' unbelievable," says a guy in a grey uniform, shaking his head. "Ya wove tru traffic and crossed all ta way to ta shoulder widout bloody front tires! Ya must 'ave some right steady 'ands on ya."

Gabhran shrugs and taps the ash from his cigarette.

"Oh, boy, do I need a snack," says Dad after we make sure everybody is okay, after all the sirens and smoke and the brand new tires.

My mother stares straight ahead. "How can you think about food at a time like this? We almost just died."

"We haven't eaten since Liverpool. Kids, don't you want some ice cream?"

I am completely miserable and exhale disgustedly, slowly, savoring it so that everyone knows. "I cannot believe I missed the dance to almost *die*, and now you're using it as an excuse to go get stupid ice cream?"

Mom scoffs. "You did not almost die."

"You just said it!"

"I did not."

"Dad, didn't she just—"

"Ice cream it is!" Dad declares, and my mother and I make an *ugh* sound and roll our eyes as we pull into a gas station.

Everyone piles out: Sax, Guitar, Bass, Drums, and Gabhran, who immediately lights up two cigarettes. Guitar reaches to grab one, but Gabhran shakes his head. He smokes them both, alternating hands, leaning against the newly dented bus.

My mother gestures to the petrol pump across the way. "Don't you think we're a little too close for comfort?"

"Reckon we've 'ad our close call fer today," Gabhran says.

It's the only sentence I've ever heard him utter, and it has the surprising power of shutting up my mother, which you usually can't do with a whole boatload full of retorts. I'm impressed.

The sky must be equally impressed because it responds almost immediately in the form of a thunderclap, followed soon after by about a hundred million raindrops. I am convinced that at least ninety million of these fall directly onto me, which I regard as more of a personal affront than a miracle of meteorological choreography. I let strands of drippy hair fall into my face and imagine an angsty power ballad playing as the camera zooms out on me doing one big "everything sucks" exhale and dramatically boarding the bus. My family is the ultimate drag.

I'm already planning the next scene of the movie when the sliding side door to the bus rudely reacquaints me with cold hard reality. The accident must have dented it, and it stubbornly refuses to reopen. This means the only ways to get in are through the front, which is jam-packed with CDs, or the back, which is full of guitars and amps and posters and other stuff we can't expose to the rain.

My mother throws up her hands and walks away. She's just *done*.

I run for cover and find the band in the little convenience store, drinking a case of beer like it's going out of style, like we're in a speakeasy or something. The whole store is filled with the sound of pop music blaring from a tinny sound system. I make my way to the bathroom and hover over a crusty toilet on tiptoe to avoid sloshing around in the layer of brown water below. While awkwardly clutching at my pants to ensure that they touch neither the toilet nor the floor, I imagine Nick Nunzio back in New York, dramatically dipping a girl much prettier than me at the climax of the slow dance. And then I see them. Three small, reddish specks. I always wondered what it would be like . . . probably some kind of ancient, secret revelation. A spiritually resonant burst of wisdom. The knowledge that everything was going to be very different from now on. Very different and very adult, and then I'd sprout awesome tits and maybe "I Am Woman" would start blaring in the background as I marched up to my mother to announce that I didn't have to take her bullshit anymore. I look closer at the specks. Hmm. Is it supposed to be this . . . unmomentous?

I am not surprised when there's no toilet paper (typical) or when the toilet doesn't flush (perfect), but I almost fall to the sticky floor when I realize that I'm locked inside the bathroom. I panic. *Shit*. I'm trapped! I pound on the door over and over again. Nobody hears. I call out. Still no answer. I'm going to die in here! HELP! I'm going to die ankle-deep in brown toilet water while the Spice Girls drown out my frantic cries for help. I'm going to—

Suddenly, the door swings open toward me. Everyone is crowded around—the band and my family and the convenience store guy holding the doorknob.

"You were pushing, love. Ta open it, yeh 'afta pull."

"Oh."

"Everything okay?" Dad asks.

"Yep."

He hands me a Twinkie, which I wolf down in two bites while beelining to the back of the store. I grab the first box of

Kotex pads I see and realize with horror that I don't have any money to pay for it.

"What's that?" my mother wants to know, appearing out of nowhere.

"Nothing."

"Show me."

"Stop it, Mom. Just leave me alone."

"What are you—" She snatches the box from behind me and pauses, smiles. Mom never ever hugs anybody, but she touches my arm affectionately. I think she might even be getting misty-eyed, but instead she grabs my hand and marches back to the bathroom, waving her hands around and shouting, "All right, people, all right! Nothing to see here." Then she discreetly tears open the box and hands me a big, fat Kotex. Actually, she's not all that discreet because everyone is still kind of watching. I am livid.

I return from the bathroom and Mom is still brandishing the offending box. *Please let me die.* Guitar and Bass extend a beer and a cigarette respectively. "Ceremonial!" Guitar explains as Mom slaps away his hand.

Maybe if I start walking now I can hitchhike my way to London and join a circus or something. Then maybe I'll finally have a normal life. Or maybe I can just walk straight into oncoming traffic and be done with it all. This is the worst part of the worst day of the worst life any girl has ever lived. All of a sudden, Sax begins to giggle, which makes Sam chuckle. Guitar chokes on a sip of beer, spitting foam all over the floor. Dad laughs out loud.

"Well, I'm glad you people are amused," I spit contemptuously.

Everyone laughs even harder. My mother, who has barely

smiled all week, is now doubled over. I am disgusted. I am furious. I am never going to speak to any of them ever again for as long as I live.

When I was little I was convinced that I had been switched at birth, that my rightful parents were living on a magical mountaintop somewhere in a resplendent palace with closets full of a million pretty dresses, waiting until the day I was old enough that they could send for me. After discovering some disappointingly graphic hospital-photo proof that I did indeed come out of my mother (the crowning of Princess Hannah?), I set my hopes on the notion that my parents were just pretending to be poor in order to keep my brother and me grounded. On the long-awaited day that I finally became a woman, they would press a button and reveal the sprawling mansion and in-ground pool hidden underneath our modest split-level ranch.

Gabhran's beard contorts in a way that I've never seen before, and I realize that even he is smiling. I will myself to remain angry, to keep my eyebrows furrowed and my arms folded. This is not what I signed up for. Nobody asked if I wanted to have a monkey for a sister or move all the way across the ocean or live in a bus with a bunch of loonies who don't listen to me and laugh hysterically at what was supposed to be my beautifully symbolic graduation from childhood. It isn't funny. Don't laugh. *Don't laugh, don't laugh, don't laugh.* But the sight of Gabhran's big furry beard-smile is too much and I can't suppress a hint of a smirk from creeping across my mouth. I hate them. And I laugh.

We stay there in the convenience store, gorging ourselves on complimentary gummy worms, balancing on cases of prawn-flavored crisps and grinning until our cheeks ache and the sun begins to rise and our minds fluff into cotton candy. The storm passes. With the rain finally stopped, we can now board through the back of the bus. We unload and reload and buckle up. Forty-nine gigs in forty-three cities to go. We pull out and I watch as the store shrinks away through the back window, along with every lingering notion of instant womanly revelations and magical mansion buttons. It's a damn shame. I guess real life doesn't work like Cinderella's. If I want the fairy tale, I'm going to have to try harder. And as we plunge into a bright swarm of headlights streaming toward the horizon, I congratulate myself on this, my first official, decidedly adult decision.

chapter three

MEAN GIRLS SUCK

I am crazy giddy with anticipation on my first day of middle school after returning from the tour. I am finally going to be a real, normal person. And I'm going to be awesome at it. Maybe one day I'll even be the princess of popular. I proudly don the patchwork jeans I made from scraps of Dublin denim, as well as a teardrop-shaped jewel with silver filigree called a bindi, affixed to the center of my forehead with a dab of eyelash glue. They're all the rage in Great Britain, and I've collected a special one from each of the different cities we visited. For today I have chosen a magenta bindi from Edinburgh, the city where I nailed a perfect saxophone solo for the first time, to give me courage.

Room 3B. I imagine the secretary who leads me in will introduce me and ask me to give a small presentation about my adventures abroad, and then I will regale the class with a song and a thrilling exhibition of my newly acquired juggling skills. But instead she leaves me there in the doorway, shouts "Keep it down in there!" and quickly departs.

Everyone stares at me, and no one says hello. Perhaps they do not want to hear me sing.

Uncomfortable with the silence, I put my head down and walk toward the back of the classroom. Most of the faces are new, but Genevieve, the most popular girl from elementary school—who by now has the biggest boobs I've ever seen on a seventh-grader—glares at me from across the way.

"What the hell is on your head?" she shouts.

I brush my hand to my cheek instinctively, fearing that perhaps there's some dirt, but another girl chimes in, "She's like one of those magic troll dolls!" I realize in a sudden rush of horror that they're talking about my beloved bindi.

"I got it in Scotland," I offer meekly as I shrink into a desk in the far corner. But there's no escaping. Genevieve and three of her friends leave their seats to gather around and inspect me further.

"Gross. It's, like, leaking. That's fugly!"

"No, that's the glue—" I try to explain.

"Eiw! She glues it on! Gluehead! Is that why your hair's all fat and huge? Do you do it with glue, too?" another asks mockingly.

"Why are your pants all patched up? Are you too poor to buy one good pair?"

I desperately look out the window, only to see that my mother's car has already pulled away.

"Look! I think Gluebaby's gonna cry! Are you gonna c—"

I run to the bathroom and tear off my stupid bindi, scraping at the remaining eyelash glue until my forehead is red and raw. I pull my hair into a tight ponytail and mentally review my wardrobe to figure out a more acceptable ensemble for the following day. I feel ugly and stupid, and most of all, upset that my triumphant return has gone so horribly awry, that the weeks of planning were all for naught. As I hear the bell, I pivot in the mirror and discover a small pink piece of paper taped to the back of my shirt. I tear it off and read the hateful words scrawled in sparkly gel pen: "Fugly Bitch."

A little heart dots the "i."

One day, Genevieve calls to tell me that "we're all wearing pink skirts to school tomorrow. It's skirt day."

I am elated that she has chosen to include me. I am also suspicious.

"Seriously!" she assures. "Listen, nobody wanted me to tell you, but you really helped me in Social Studies yesterday, so I figured I would warn you so you don't look totally fugly tomorrow. Okay?"

A careful inspection of my closet reveals that I have absolutely nothing to wear.

"Ma, I hate my clothes," I lament dolefully.

"But we went shopping before you started school!"

"I know, but it's all fugly."

"Excuse me?"

"It's *fugly*. I need a skirt."

My mother looks disappointed, like the time I told her I'd rather be eaten alive by fire ants than be seen with her and my father at the movies. It seems I am on my own.

"Fine," I huff, as I tromp into my room and dump out all the allowance money I've saved up. Twenty-six dollars. I walk the half-hour it takes to reach the shopping center and try on what seems like a million different skirts, all wrong, all horrible. Finally, I find a short cotton one with a groovy floral pattern and a scalloped hem and reluctantly spend everything I've got.

The next morning I put on my beautiful skirt and twirl around in the mirror until I am dizzy. "Oh, it's just something I picked up," I imagine telling the girls. I practically prance all the way from my locker to Room 3B, eagerly anticipating my grand entrance, until I open the door and my heart sinks. Genevieve, clad in tight blue jeans along with every other girl in the class, points at me and shrieks.

"She actually did it! *Look* at that fugly pink thing!"

I am only halfway to the bathroom when the tears come. I huddle in the farthest stall and sob right through the first bell, morning announcements, and the Pledge of Allegiance. When the hall is clear, I sneak to the nurse's office.

"I need to go home."

"Are you sick?"

"I need to go home," I insist.

"Well, let's take your temperatu—"

"Please, can I just call my mom?"

"What's wrong with you, dear?" she asks.

I clutch at my stupid skirt and feel ashamed as a fat tear rolls down my cheek. I close my eyes to think, but before I can even begin to process, I hear myself reply, "Everything."

"Hannah, tell me more about plate tectonics!" I imagine Nick Nunzio saying after I wow my Earth Science class with a stellar explanation of Pangaea. I've already covered this year's entire curriculum and then some while being home-schooled, but excitedly waving my hand in the air whenever I know the answer to a question somehow does not win me as many friends and admirers as I had anticipated. If you want to impress a popular middle-school guy, you don't wax poetic about continental drift. Nick completely ignores me.

If you want to survive the day, you don't try so hard to impress Nick Nunzio. I come home with a black eye.

"That's it!" Mom says. "We're taking you out. I never thought I'd say this, but your father was right."

"No! I don't want to be home-schooled again!"

"Hannah, we—"

"No, *please*! I'll never make any friends. I'll be like those weird kids with greasy hair who talk to themselves onstage in the National Spelling Bee!"

"Hannah, it just doesn't seem like you—"

"Mom, I'm *trying*!"

And I am. I'm trying to stop raising my hand so much, even when I know the answer. I'm trying to fit in by wearing turquoise eye shadow and gelling my hair into a ponytail and shopping for tight tops and track pants at the Salvation Army. I'm also experimenting with different types of padding for my training bra. The tissues fell out one day at recess, which was almost a total disaster, and the ankle socks just looked lumpy, but I'm getting a lot of mileage out of sculpted Play-Doh covered in Saran Wrap.

"Ooh, are we molding cartoon aliens?!" Dad exclaims upon seeing the bra-padding operation. He picks up a hunk of yellow clay and rolls it into a worm. "Look! A tentacle! Do you need help sculpting ears? Because I always had trouble with the ea—"

"No, Dad, get OUT!"

He seems insulted and I feel kind of bad, but not as bad as the next day when I come back from gym class to find my locker open and my bra overturned to reveal two horrible yellow smiley faces. Someone has reshaped the Play-Doh. *Shit.*

I'm changing clothes as fast as I can, wishing I were invisible, when Genevieve and the rest of the popular clique saunter over.

"We weren't sure if we should call you Toddler Tits from now on, or *Flat* Monkey-Girl Freak. What do you think?"

When I complain to my parents that the girls are chucking carrot sticks at me during lunch, Dad tries to comfort me: "If you just try to be yourself, things will turn out eventually."

I hate it when he talks like a fortune cookie. "Turn out *how*?"

"Somehow. Things always turn out somehow." He smiles.

"Dad, that doesn't even make any *sense*!"

Mom looks up from her address book. "She's right, Dean. That doesn't make any sense. Hannah, what you really need to do is—" She snaps the book closed. "Well, who is their leader?"

"What do you mean?"

"The meanest girl."

"Genevieve."

"What you really need to do is take out their leader." All of Mom's social insights are drawn from her knowledge of troop hierarchy in the animal kingdom.

"How do I do that?"

"Oh, you know. Intimidation, humiliation, brute strength . . . there are a lot of—"

"Alison, what are you talking about?" Dad interjects. "That's sick! She's thirteen!"

"This is war, Dean. First it's carrots, next thing you know it'll be pizza and pudding. You have to nip this in the bud, sweetie."

"But what if I get in trouble?"

"The administration seems much more concerned with making you take standardized tests than making sure you aren't being tortured. Sometimes you just have to fight fire with fire."

Dad waves his hands. "No, no, no, wait a minute. You never fight fire with fire! That just makes one enormous, out-of-control fire!"

"Well, what do you propose?"

"How about using water? Defuse the situation." Dad goes to the fridge to retrieve a slice of lemon meringue pie and returns with two forks. "Why don't you go tell these girls how much it hurts your feelings when they tease you, that you have a lot in common, and that you'd like them to stop." And then he adds playfully, "Or else you'll punch 'em in the nose."

"Actually, that might not be a bad idea," Mom says. "They certainly wouldn't see it coming . . ."

The next day, I am hit in the head with carrot stick number five, catapulted over from the popular table. With my mom's advice ringing in my ears, I pick up my carton of chocolate milk and dump it all over Genevieve's head. It feels amazing. People cheer. Unfortunately, I do not know that she has a severe milk allergy, and I spend the next three weeks in detention.

Mom decides that if I can get a scholarship, then I'm going to private school. I think this is a marvelous idea. I realize that the problem with middle school is that people still remember me from before I left for Great Britain. A new school would mean all new people, none of whom know anything about the monkey, the Shoe Car, the bindi, the Play-Doh, or my chocolate milk misdemeanor. I decide that the new Hannah, the completely new and improved Hannah, will be neither fugly nor a freak. Now I know how to play the game . . . and I'm going to kick butt in round two.

chapter four

PRIVATE SCHOOL SUCKS

Biltmore Collegiate is one of the most prestigious schools in New York State. My parents drive me to my interview, and as we approach the medieval-looking campus, identical plaid dots appear to be swarming all over. I realize they are uniformed students. The place reminds me of a fancy ant farm—studious kids in neat little rows with pleated skirts and ties and bows, all darting across the pristinely manicured lawns with intense focus. Unlike in public school, there are no rogue stripes of blue hair, no torn jeans, no dirty sneakers. There is not so much as a stray ear piercing, let alone a gaudy nose ring situation.

In the admissions office, I am told by a stodgy man with a starched bowtie that all hair must conform to dress code. "No unnatural tints. Boys' hair must not extend lower than the top of the dress shirt collar, on penalty of suspension," he declares proudly, as if showing off the amenities in a new luxury condominium.

I notice my mother tugging reflexively at her right earlobe.

She's wearing the fake diamond earrings that look impressive but are too heavy for her small ears. I am led out of the office and into the hallway to meet my student tour guide. Lost in a sea of plaid and pearls, I become painfully aware of my shabby shoes. I stare in disgust at the frayed laces and scuffed heels. I hope nobody—

"I'm Swan." An assertive, perfectly manicured hand extends toward me.

Swan has the whitest teeth I've ever seen, even whiter than the shellacked Giant Tap Dancing Teeth Costume. She motions for me to follow her as she sashays primly down the hall.

"Status?" she asks without turning.

"What?"

"Prospective? Admit? Legacy?" She whips around for a beat to consider me, appraising with a calculated stare. "*Not* legacy?"

"Oh. Um, I'm looking at Biltmore. Prospective."

I bump into Swan as she stops short and then steps to the side, tugging at the bottom of her skirt. She eyes a crowd of students and teachers walking by. "False alarm," she explains, rolling the skirt at the waistband. "Fold and flip. When administration walks by, you pull down from the knee and you're back in dress code: *voilà!*" she demonstrates.

I nod as if I'm getting battle advice from Napoleon himself and make a mental note. Buck system. Short skirts.

"C'mon, off to Latin," she announces. Her short plaid pleats sway sassily as she disappears around a corner. An obnoxiously loud bell brings forth a flood of uniformed students, and I have to pay close attention to keep track of Swan's bobbing ponytail as she navigates crowded dark corridors lined with marble busts and antique gilded picture frames.

Long ago I resigned myself to the fact that school isn't supposed to be interesting, so even though the lesson plans in the classes I visit are dreary, I'm just impressed that the kids bother to raise their hands at all. When they speak, they're eloquent and insightful. They all take notes and nobody throws spitballs or tries to fashion makeshift weapons out of three-ring binders when the teacher's back is turned. I could get used to this.

Swan does not say good-bye, does not even turn to acknowledge me when she drops me off at the admissions office, where I meet back up with my parents. They fidget nervously. It's time for the interview.

The head of admissions is a stately woman in a gray pantsuit with enormous shoulder pads. She peruses my file and, without looking up, asks, "What is the name of the brand of your acoustic guitar?"

I am caught off-guard and feel like a fraud immediately. If I were a real musician, I'd know this. I bite my lip, feel my cheeks getting hot, and look to Dad, who mouths the name.

"Yamaha!" I say.

She squints a bit, jots something down, and nods. "And it says here you like to read. Which five authors have had the greatest impact on your evolving literary consciousness?"

My confidence dwindles as I frantically grasp for worthy names, like Twain and Woolf. I skip over authors who seem too frivolous or modern, trying desperately to imagine how my answers will sound before I give them. After a few more terrifying questions, the woman seems satisfied. She closes the file.

"Your daughter's test scores are exceptional," the woman concludes. "But is she truly Biltmore material?"

Dad clears his throat. "Well, uh, Hannah's always, um . . . she's very academically curious, and—"

The woman holds up her finger. "Rhetorical question," she corrects. "The committee will let you know in a few weeks. Thank you very much for your time."

With that, she shoos us out the door, and we walk to the car in silence. I think about Swan and the plaid uniforms and the admissions lady with prickly puzzlement as we pull out of the parking lot and drive away from the forbidding stone castle of a school. As much as I don't like that admissions lady, I really want her to like me. I want her to think that I am "Biltmore material."

As soon as the campus is in our rearview mirror, Mom pulls out her earrings, kicks off her shoes, and shimmies out of her stockings. She puts her naked feet up on the dashboard and sighs, stretching. "What. A. Bitch."

I visit half a dozen more private schools before I fall in love. Danforth Academy has no uniforms, and even though the kids are wealthy, I don't feel nearly as out of place on the tour as I did at Biltmore. The classrooms are bright and airy, with big oval tables. The students seem genuinely happy, and they all gather at the beginning of the day for a Morning Meeting where people sing songs and do skits and talk about community service. It's perfect.

Mom nods. "And this decision has absolutely nothing to do with the fact that there is an out-and-out palace on campus?"

I gasp because I am *horrified*. "What are you even *talking* about?"

"Hannah, I just don't want a repeat of the glitter-ribbon-rainbow shoes."

When I was six years old, I fell in love with the most fantastically fabulous, glittery rainbow shoes in the whole wide world, which had ribbons for laces, and which my mother insisted were poorly made even though I assured her they were the most comfortable shoes *ever*. I wore them everyday. Sometimes I didn't even take them off to sleep. However, in addition to being extremely poorly made, they also had the tendency to cut into my anklebone like a glitter-ribbon-rainbow dagger. This resulted in a half princess-glide, half penguin-waddle that led my first-grade teacher to assume I was physically challenged.

"Mrs. Friedman, every child has special needs. Hannah's might just be a little *extra* special."

"How many times do I have to tell you? Hannah is not disabled! She's just stubborn. I knew those damn shoes were a mistake . . . "

Mom puts down the Danforth Academy catalogue she has been flipping through and eyes me probingly. "So you're sure you like this one?"

"It's perfect. I can feel it."

"You know you'd have to get a weekend job to cover the cost of books? And you're okay with the long commute? And you realize these kids would be just as loaded as the ones at Biltmore?"

"Yes, yes, yesss."

She reaches behind her and plops a fat envelope down onto the table. "Well, then, congratulations. You got in last week."

"What?!"

"I wanted to make sure you had considered everything carefully."

"I got in? I'm going?!"

"You're going. And even with the scholarship you're going to put your father and me into more debt than we ever thought possible, so you'd better appreciate it."

Later that evening, I flip idly through the glossy catalogue. I see myself debating important philosophical theories around the beautiful wooden tables. I see myself painting in the gorgeous art building and performing onstage in the plush auditorium and laughing at a hilarious joke while surrounded by friends in the cafeteria, which they call a "dining hall." How fancy is that?

And even though it had absolutely zero influence, not even a molecule of an effect on my decision, I stare at pictures of Rosewood Palace. Technically it's in the style of a *château*, but compared to my middle school, what with all its exposed wires and rusted pipes in the ceiling, it might as well be Cinderella's castle.

Actually, it's better.

When I was eight, my family visited Disney World. After a few loopy rides and some pictures with Mickey we were caught in a torrential rainstorm, but I insisted that we could not leave without going to the Magic Kingdom to see Cinderella's castle—the one in the Disney logo. The ultimate icon of childhood wonderment, it embodied all of my little girl dreams within its tulip-shaped turrets and sparkling moat. Every time I watched *Aladdin* or *The Little Mermaid* and the castle emerged in the credit sequence from behind a twinkling cloud to the tune of "When You Wish Upon a Star," I felt certain that dreams really did come true, and that if only I wished hard enough, one day I would live inside that castle and be the princess of the whole wide world.

The castle was a lot smaller in person, even for a small person like me. There were no grand ballrooms or golden spinning wheels or dancing mice darning dresses, only a hollowed-out tunnel you could walk through with some lame pictures on the walls. This was not right. This was not my fairy tale. I left Disney World feeling dejected and lied to, convinced that somewhere out there, they were hiding the *real deal*. It probably wasn't for any old tourist to gawk at. Maybe you had to earn it.

When my tour guide at Danforth Academy showed me Rosewood Palace, where special events were held, I thought I had died and gone to Pretty Pretty Princess Heaven. This was part of a *school?* The magnificent gardens, the marble columns, the octagonal ballroom with stained-glass windows shining dappled light across the glossy patterned oak floor? There was even a princess staircase, just like in *Beauty and the Beast* . . . I imagined myself in a golden ball gown gliding down its elegant pink marble steps with the grace of a cherry blossom.

This was it.

The night before I start high school at Danforth Academy, I write myself a wish list. I stopped believing in magic a few months ago when I did a love spell on Nick Nunzio and then he pulled me aside after math to say, "Hey, can you do me a huge favor and ask out Genevieve for me?" And then he sneezed in my face. And laughed. If I do have some kind of benevolent fairy person looking out for me, she's doing a pretty crappy job. But even so, maybe this whole Danforth Academy thing means that things are finally looking up. And on the one-in-a-zillion chance that the universe is actually listening, I figure I should give it some guidelines.

Dear universe,

As you are probably aware, I am starting a new school tomorrow. And I know that's not super important. I know there are kids starving in Africa and everything. And I know you can't just wave a magic wand and make things happen. But I was hoping you might consider giving me some tips on how to fix myself so that I can get these things:

1. I want lots of friends. I'm not picky, but preferably lots of nice, smart, fun friends who like to sleep over at my house and play games and watch movies and write songs and who don't like monkeys.

2. I want a boyfriend. I want boobs like Genevieve's, and I want to get these stupid braces off and have white, white teeth like Swan and wear cool clothes and listen to cool music and have a handsome, funny boyfriend who is madly in LOVE with me. I want to be in love.

3. I want to be cool. I know this might be like a genetic impossibility, but can we at least make me cooler?

I'll give up my allowance forever. I'll give you my next four birthday wishes, plus every shooting star I ever see. I'll do whatever it takes. I'll even give you the monkey.

Thank you in advance.

Yours wishfully,
Hannah Friedman

chapter five

FITTING IN SUCKS

On the first day of high school, I'm waiting nervously at the train platform when I spot a guy I recognize from the tour. He's gorgeous, with dark hair and azure eyes, and he wears a distinctive smirk. I try to act nonchalant, but maybe I'm being too nonchalant because he doesn't seem to notice me at all. I have to be brave. I extend my hand assertively like Swan and wrack my brain for a spectacular opening line.

"I'm Hannah."

"Julian."

"I'm new." Silence. "So . . . I guess we'll be taking the train together a lot, huh?"

"Sorry to hear it," he mumbles out of the corner of his mouth, then raises one eyebrow dramatically as if the left side of his face is appalled by what the right has just said. "Sorry to hear you'll be *train*-ing it," he clarifies. "Not sorry about the—never mind. Anyway, quick tip: keep an eye out for the sleazy guy in the overcoat who jacks off to pretty girls."

"Okay." *Did he just call me pretty?*

He straightens up and tugs at the collar of his shirt. Then, in an ironic voice that sounds like a 1970s TV game-show host, he says, "So, tell me a little about yourself, Hannah."

Be cool. "Well, um, my dad's a musician. And my mom—" I am about to tell him about Amelia, but I stop myself.

Julian picks up where I left off. "Well, my old man's a high-functioning alcoholic, and I'm fairly certain the only reason my mother calls me 'son' is because she can't tell me and my brother apart. But I didn't ask you about your family. I asked about you."

"I . . . " like musical theater? What the heck am I supposed to say?

"You better think about it before we get up to school, doll. Wouldn't want a nice girl like you getting mixed up with the Great Eight or something."

History class. It's quiet. I find a seat and turn my notebook to the first page—blank, white, brand new. Two minutes past the hour and still no sign of the teacher. *Hmm.* I curl my toes and squeeze my knees together, looking around the table at the neat collared shirts, the foot tapping, the pen twirling. I realize that everyone else looks a little nervous, too. Here is my chance. Julian asked about *me*, and here is my chance to showcase the new and improved version. The one who isn't socially retarded like her parents. Summoning all my courage, I take a deep breath and announce, "So, does anybody have funny summer stories?"

No one says anything and I feel like a giant, blaring failure. *Idiot.* Then a goofy kid in a black bowler who reminds me of Felix the Cat breaks the silence.

"I was in a hurricane," he offers.

"No way!" I say. And just like that, the whole class is chatting and laughing about their adventures with boats and beaches and backyard barbecues.

After class, a thin, pale girl in a pink cashmere sweater taps me on the shoulder.

"Hey, that was cool back there," she says. "I was dying of boredom."

"Yeah, me, too." I roll my eyes like she does.

Cashmere's strawberry-blonde hair is swept back in a flawless bun. She carries a cream- and rose-colored tote, which cannot possibly contain anything larger than a cell phone and lip gloss. She does something amazing. She invites me to her birthday party. *Aaaah!*

Afterward I go into the bathroom and do a jumping, arm-flailing, hooray-hooray-hooray victory dance until someone comes out of a seemingly empty stall. I quickly pretend to be itching my arm. I look at myself in the mirror and itch and grin.

New Hannah, 1. Nerd Hannah, 0.

Cashmere's party is a sleepover, which I'm nervous about. I do not like sleepovers. Ever since I saw a movie called *Demonic Toys* in which shark-toothed teddy bears and evil red-eyed baby dolls go around eating people's faces off, I haven't trusted other kids' rooms not to come to life and try to kill me. The idea of being the last one awake sends me into a panic, because I know that person is always the one who gets abducted by the poltergeist.

It doesn't help matters that when I was little, my grandmother decided that my parents were bad, non-observant Jews, and that it was up to her to teach me all about the history of our people. To Bubby, the Holocaust was a perfectly appropriate bedtime story. Rape, murder, and tragedy of all kinds were also fair game, which led to a very confusing chunk of time when I staged a breakfast boycott because I was concerned that the "cereal killers" might have poisoned it. I refused to attend gymnastics if my dad had a sip of apple juice because he would be "drinking and driving." And once I had to explain to my second-grade English teacher that, no, I didn't misspell the word "program," I really did mean to write, "Sally had a very bad time at yesterday's *pogrom.*"

Family neuroses, coupled with my overactive imagination, result in many sleepless nights during which I am absolutely convinced that evil ghosts, brain-sucking aliens, or mass-murdering psychozombies are lurking just behind that fluttering curtain, waiting to pounce. I am haunted by the *Scary Stories* tale about a woman with a pencil-prick dot on her arm that grows into a giant, pulsating gray lump. One day it bursts open and thousands of baby spiders pour out. I inspect every pinprick blemish with the horrified certainty that it's a spider-incubating boil, or a tumor, or both. I don't like confined spaces or big crowds or payphone change return slots, because once I read that people put needles inside them contaminated with HIV.

In my own house, I have identified the quickest way to get up on the roof in case of a volcano, and down to the basement in case of a tornado. And I know all the best secret hiding places in case vampires are looking for me. Or Nazis. Sometimes I pretend I am Anne Frank and curl up my legs and hide in my closet to see how quietly I can breathe and how long I can manage to stay in the pitch black before I have to blow my cover. It's usually not very long, because it turns out that the dark is scarier than the Nazis. At least you can see the Nazis.

Cashmere lives near school, almost an hour away from my house, so I know I can't call my parents to come pick me up if I have a stomach-achy panic attack like I do at most sleep-over attempts. *What if I'm the last one awake?*
"You'll read a book," Mom says.
"What if I get sick?"
"You'll take some Pepto-Bismol."
"But what if I—"
"Hannah, you're going to be fine. Don't you think you're getting a little old for this sleepover phobia?"
Of course I do, but thinking about this just makes me ashamed, and so I prefer not to. I have scoured the advice sections of teen magazines, searching for people similarly afflicted with this annoying sleepover-itis, but I haven't found anything and so I've concluded that I'm just a big crybaby who will have to attend college via teleconference.

Mom drives me to Cashmere's house. We get there early and I beg her to drive around the block for a few laps so I'm not the first kid there.
"What am I, your chauffeur? I have errands to do." She parks and grabs my duffel from the back. "What the hell is in here, railroad spikes? You're staying one night!"
"I didn't want to forget anything."
We knock. A birdlike blonde woman in a crisp lavender dress and pointy-toed black heels greets us. "Darlings!

Welcome, welcome. I'm Dot! Dotty for short."

"Nice to meet you. I'm—"

"And you must be Anne! And mother of Anne!"

"Hannah," I correct politely.

"Anne and Hannah. Isn't that just *adorable.*"

Suddenly, we are besieged by a pack of small, yippy dogs that weave in frantic formation, sniffing, leaping, and biting each other's tails. Each sports a silk hair bow of a different color. Their frenetic energy is redoubled in a floor-to-ceiling mirror with an extravagant gold frame. I check my hair. It seems frazzled.

Dot looks frazzled, too. "Lupita!"

One of the dogs knocks over a black lacquered umbrella stand, which clatters noisily on the marble floor.

"Terribly sorry. Just a moment." I can see her scowling in the mirror as she scurries up the stairs. "Lu-piii-ta!"

Mom nudges me. "How does she walk in those *witch* shoes?" she whispers.

I giggle.

Dot returns with a hundred-watt smile and a tired-looking, dark-haired woman who shoos all the dogs up the stairs in a final flurry of yips and fur. "Excitable little scamps," Dot laughs. "Come, come, let's get you settled!"

We follow Dot through a maze of rooms that seem to have come straight out of an interior-design magazine—bold black and crimson velvet wallpaper, twisting amorphous glass sculptures, an entire room filled only with fine china behind glass display cases. We arrive at a sumptuous purple couch covered with twenty or thirty tiny pillows opposite a ginormous television.

"The girls will be sleeping in here, Anne."

"Hannah."

"Everything will be supervised, of course," she assures my mother. She turns to eye me sternly. "And we absolutely do *not* tolerate intoxicants or unruliness in this house."

"Good thing we left all those intoxicants out in the car, huh?" Mom jokes.

"Aha." Dot purses her lips in disapproval, and suddenly I am desperate for my mother to leave.

"Have you met any of the other parents?" Dot asks her.

"A few, at that weekend reception thing. Everyone was very friendly. The Hunts—"

Dot rolls her eyes. "Third wife. He left the first one for the babysitter and the second one for the nanny. Next thing you know, he'll be running off with the *pool boy*, if you know what I mean." She claps her hands excitedly. "Who else, who else?"

"The, the Delgados?"

"Oh, Ted is a doll, but Julie is an absolute *loon*. Last year, she took five months off from the Arts Council—she said it was to visit her sister, but everyone knew she was in rehab. Not that there's anything *wrong* with rehab, you understand, it's just that I appreciate when people are *honest* about their problems instead of expecting me to believe these absurd little *lies*. Like when Kate disappeared from PTA meetings for four weeks and had all her meals delivered to her house and then came back looking ten years younger and telling everyone it was yoga and macrobiotic *food!* Macrobiotic food, my foot. I mean, am I right or am I *right?*"

"You are *absolutely right*," Mom declares. I wonder if Dot detects the heavy sarcasm.

Once Mom finally leaves, Dot rests her hand on my knee. "I'm so glad you and Cashmere have become friends. Your mother told me on the phone all about the . . . *issues* at your old school, and I want you to know that you are *safe* here."

I make a mental note to kill my mother.

"Your mother seems lovely," says Dot. "And her breasts are fantastic. How long has she had them?"

I am flabbergasted. "Um, always?"

She nods knowingly. "They say one in fifty of those old silicone jobs just lasts *forever.* Nowadays," she pushes up her boobs, "they keep you coming back for more."

"Who are *you?*" asks a tiny blonde wearing diamond studs approximately the size of Rhode Island. I think her name starts with a B.

"I'm Hannah."

"Ohmi*god,* you're that new girl! Kisses!" she exclaims, grabbing me by the shoulders and air-kissing both cheeks.

Two more Bs arrive. Brooke? Bridget? I can't keep track.

"You are such a whore," one of them laughs, throwing a pillow at a willowy brunette with a turned-up nose. I recognize her from class. Teagan, I think.

"Well, hello to you, too," Teagan snaps, tossing her hair. "Where's Lupita? I'm starving."

"I'm *shocked,*" one of the Bs replies sarcastically, smacking Teagan on her tiny bottom. "What's your Gram giving you now?"

"I get a thousand bucks for every five pounds I lose. I've been saving up calories, like, all week for this party. Hey! New girl!" she says upon seeing me.

"This is *so* exciting!" says another one of the Bs. "It's about time we had some new blood. I was starting to feel like we'd be *inbred* by junior year."

"Wait . . . what?" Teagan asks, puzzled.

"Don't think too hard, Tea," a B quips, "it'll give you wrinkles."

"Whatever," Teagan replies, getting out a compact and inspecting her face.

Lupita enters, balancing three large silver trays loaded with the most plentiful spread of junk food I've ever seen: towers of warm fresh-baked pita with red pepper hummus and olive tapenade, homemade oatmeal raisin cookies, and an entire pyramid of fresh fruit with dark chocolate fondue. Someone turns on MTV. We critique.

"Eiw, I do *not* get why people like Christina Aguilera. She's such a slut."

"I know, right?"

"Ya, but she's a way better singer than Britney."

"At least Britney has some class."

"Ya, and Old Navy is fucking *haute couture!*" one of the Bs hollers.

Everybody laughs riotously. I laugh right along with them, but secretly I am super-relieved that my neurotic overpacking included an extra sleeping shirt. The Old Navy one will clearly not be making an appearance tonight.

Dot is clapping her hands frantically in the doorway. "Attention, ladies! Attention!" She puts her finger to her lips, and everybody stops talking. I wonder what's going on. Dot dims the lights. Lupita emerges from behind the ornate French doors carrying a four-tiered lavender cake covered in delicate buttercream rosebuds. It's beautiful. And suddenly I realize Cashmere is nowhere to be seen. In fact, she has yet to make even a single appearance at her own party. We wait in silence. Then Dot gestures grandly to the staircase.

There stands Cashmere, pretty as a picture, perfectly poised on the top step like a daffodil ballerina, sheer yellow chiffon petals billowing just above her knees. She descends slowly, gracefully, as we sing *Happy Birthday*, covering her mouth as if to show embarrassment, as if she never intended for anyone to make such a fuss. Illuminated by the soft glow of the tiny pink candles, Cashmere demurely ponders her birthday wish with closed eyes and an angelic smile.

Dot kisses her on the cheek. They pose for a picture. Cashmere blows out her fifteen candles, and we can't help but clap.

It's absolutely perfect.

After her grand entrance, Cashmere changes into pajamas and joins the party. We make up silly dances and eat way too much ice cream and take pictures of ourselves wearing Cashmere's mother's mink stoles. The girls ask me all sorts of questions, and I find myself telling stories about middle school—about Genevieve and her many suitors and her crazy parties.

Except that in the stories, Genevieve is me.

The girls are rehashing a vast repertoire of inside jokes from years past, none of which I understand. "Remember the *sheep*?" means absolutely nothing to me, though everyone else collapses in stitches on the floor. Apparently "Ohmigod, I saw Charles in the coffee shop talking to *Margaret!*" is the most shocking announcement anybody has ever heard. I pretend to be surprised.

"Hey, where *is* Margaret?" Teagan gasps as the laughter subsides.

"Duh," Cashmere smirks, gesturing to me like a prize thoroughbred. "She's been bumped."

One of the Bs shakes her head. "Um, we have *not* discussed replacements yet."

Cashmere isn't listening. She's focused on a computer screen across the room. "Ohmigod, no *way*. She's online."

Everyone crowds around as Cashmere logs out of her instant messenger account and logs back in under a new screen name.

"This is my *other* account," she explains.

Teagan cocks her head. "But won't she know it's—"

"'C' could just as easily be for Charles," Cashmere explains matter-of-factly.

> **CC04:** hey margaret, whats up?
> **LilMissM:** whos this?
> **CC04:** Charles

"Aaah! Tell her you, like, want to have a *threesome* with her!" Teagan suggests enthusiastically.

"No, you *idiot*, that would give us away," Cashmere says coldly. "Now shut up. I'm thinking."

> **CC04:** had fun catching up the other day
> **LilMissM:** ya, me 2. Glad to be past last year's drama

"That little bitch!" a B shouts.

"Margaret is, like, totally evil," Teagan tells me. "Last year she told the middle school dean that Cashmere and Charles were—"

"Shut *up*, Teagan," Cashmere snaps, tapping her nails on the keyboard. "Ah, here we go. I'm a *genius*."

> **CC04:** Listen, i think u should run for class prez @ the mting next Fri. srsly. Im running again- itd b fun 2 do it 2gether.

The girls shriek with glee. "You think she'll buy it?" the B with braces asks.

> **LilMissM:** u know what? mayb i will!

"Bought and gift wrapped," Cashmere smiles smugly.

By the time heads begin to hit pillows, I am suddenly seized by a familiar panic. Fire. Aliens. *Last one awake!* But calling my parents to come pick me up would be unthinkable, social suicide, and I do feel pretty tired. I look around at my new friends sprawled all over the gorgeous Oriental rug and realize that New Hannah does not have time for freaking out about sleepovers. I stop wondering if I'll be okay and decide that I just will be. I have to be.

To my great surprise, after a million stomachaches and embarrassing 2 AM calls to my mother, this seems to be the deceptively simple cure. I awaken triumphantly the next morning to the smell of fresh pancakes. No aliens, no fires, no Nazis. All that time I spent worrying about the worst-case scenario had created a worst-case scenario. I. Am. Awesome.

Until the following Friday, of course, when I. Am. Screwed.

A chubby girl with dirty blonde hair and an enormous, angry red pimple the size of a quarter on her forehead is standing up in front of the whole grade at the Morning Meeting. Teagan is trying to stop herself from laughing by chewing on her hair. Judging by the self-satisfied look on Cashmere's face, I assume that this chubby girl must be Margaret. She's not what I expected. I figured she would rival Cashmere in looks or at least in style to warrant such ire, but her dorkiness is so cringingly obvious that even *I* can smell it from across the room.

"And who will be seconding Margaret's presidential nomination?" asks the teacher running the meeting.

Margaret looks pleadingly at Charles. She fidgets, watching him, but he seems not to notice her at all. She stands facing the sea of silent judgment that is our freshman class, growing paler by the minute. Nobody is going to second her. It's pitiful. I can't take it anymore. I raise my hand.

"Great. You there . . . "

"Hannah."

"Hannah. Okay. And who will be seconding *your* presidential nomination?"

Seconding? "Oh, no, I just meant to—"

Cashmere shoots me a look and my jaw clamps shut. If I admit I was trying to save Margaret, I might become the next target of instant message duplicity. I wish I could disappear out the library doors. I need a plan. Fake a heart attack? Everyone is staring. *Shit.* I steel myself and walk across the room to join Margaret onstage, desperately scanning the crowd, hoping someone will raise a hand. Cashmere looks amused as she leans back, pursing her glossy pink lips, reveling.

The teacher sighs. "Does *any*body second Hannah's bid?"

Time grinds to a halt. I'm going to crack. *Fuck.*

Just then the silence is broken by the sound of footsteps as Julian ambles into the auditorium, clutching a cup of coffee. The teacher stares at him disapprovingly as he settles into a chair in the front row. The teacher shakes his head and crosses his arms, waiting for an explanation.

Julian is completely unruffled. "Did I miss anything good?"

"You are interrupting presidential nominations, Julian."

"And here I thought I had timed my entrance so perfectly."

"Your con*tinued* disruptions are postponing the entire process."

"My most sincere apologies, sir."

Silence. Lots of it.

Julian looks at the teacher expectantly. "So, are we waiting for . . . Godot?"

"We are waiting for someone to second the nominations of—"

Julian smiles. "I second her," he says, pointing to me and winking. "And her." He points to Margaret. "Everyone. I second all of them."

A kid in the back row wearing a giant green jacket who I recognize from the train jumps up and shouts, "Down with the oligarchy!"

Everyone laughs as the teacher shakes his head again and adjourns the meeting.

I catch up to Julian in the hallway and tap him on the shoulder. "Hey, thanks. You kind of saved my life back there."

"Oh." His left eye twitches a bit. "No problem, toots."

Every time I consider rescinding my bid, something stops me. *What if I actually win?* It would be the ultimate proof that New Hannah isn't just wishful thinking. The thought of announcing triumphantly to my parents that "I'm class president!" keeps me writing speech drafts long after I want to quit. If I win, it'll show how much I deserve to be at Danforth, how much I appreciate it, how much better I already am.

I practice my speech in front of the mirror every night. The morning of the election, I take the early train to make sure I get there in plenty of time. I sit in the dining hall nursing a cup of coffee, reviewing my notecards over and over and over. Now or never.

When it's finally my turn to speak, my breath feels short and I stammer a "H-hi, my n-name is Hannah." But slowly, I lose myself in the flow of the familiar words, and by the time the voice in my head starts to wonder, *Do they think you're totally full of shit and your hair looks like a squirrel's nest?* I am already done. People clap. It's weird.

At the end of the day, an election announcement is posted on a board in the main hall. I tell myself that I tried my best and it was a good experience and all the rest of those lame things you say to yourself when you know you're really just a big fat loser.

But then I realize that the name on the board is mine. I won. I actually won.

This affords me no small amount of pride until I tell my parents, who do not give me the reaction I was hoping for.

"So you volunteered?" my mother wonders.

"No, Mom, I won."

"Like in a lottery?"

"No, I *won!* People voted!"

Dad pats me on the head. "Well, congratulations, honey bunny! That's amazing."

"What do you mean, 'that's amazing'? You didn't think I could win?"

"Of course not, sweet potato! We knew you could win. We just didn't think you *would.*"

I stare at them both in disbelief and then storm off to my room, making sure to stamp as loudly as possible. Then I slam the door twice before locking it.

The next day at school Cashmere sidles up to me, followed closely by Teagan, the Bs, and the rest of the Great Eight. I brace myself. They haven't mentioned the whole Margaret thing all week. I prepare for the worst.

"Didn't know you had political aspirations, Hannz."

She called me Hannz! Wait . . . is that good? "Yeah, it was sort of a last-minute thing."

"It'll be nice to have one of us in office," Cashmere declares.

Teagan purses her pouty lips and starts ticking off points in the air. "We wanna, like, bring back the freshman fashion show, and we want uniforms for spirit squad, and *no* summer reading, and, like, Diet Coke in the soda machines."

"Oh. Well, I'll certainly try."

Cashmere smiles, draping an arm across my shoulder possessively. "Congrats, Madame President." The other girls gather around in a tight circle.

One of the Bs smacks my ass. "Welcome to the Great Eight, Hannz."

chapter six

FRIENDS SUCK

Cashmere's sprawling mansion and Teagan's vast purse collection are the envy of every girl in school, but even so, the most perfect person at Danforth, hands down, is Scarlet Karr. Rich and blonde, she has the best of every requisite popular-girl accessory: the newest designer purses, the trendiest fashions, and the finest French perfumes. She even has a gorgeous *college* boyfriend who sends roses to her dorm room and croons original romantic songs on her voicemail, which she eagerly replays on her Swarovski crystal-coated cell phone, making every girl in earshot crazy with jealousy. After transferring from California for her junior year, it takes her only a month to rise from total anonymity to social royalty. She wins the lead in the school musical and a seat at the most popular lunch table while attracting the lust of every straight guy and the cultish adoration of the girls and the gays. She is the Madonna of Danforth Academy, and with each $300 haircut and weekend trip to St. Lucia, she cements her status as our very own tabloid queen.

"Did you hear that Scarlet was at Nobu this weekend? I heard that Brad Pitt came up to her and said she was the most gorgeous girl in the room and bought her a drink and asked if she wanted to go with him to a *soirée*. At *Sarah Jessica Parker's* house! But she couldn't go because she had already been invited to the MTV Movie Awards after party!"

"Well, I heard she took a rain check and he's flying her out to the Hamptons next month."

"You don't need to fly to the Hamptons from New York!"

"But you would if you had a private helicopter."

Unlike a lot of the ditzy heiress types, Scarlet has brains, which only makes her even more maddeningly perfect. She's always ready with the perfect witty quip. Whenever I lose my train of thought, I try to imagine what Scarlet would say. She's like one of those people in the movies who always has the perfect comeback, except she doesn't have a script. She's spectacular all on her own.

As if I didn't have enough of an inferiority complex around Scarlet, a few weeks into rehearsals for the musical, the universe pulls one majorly sick joke. Near the end of the show, Scarlet performs a comic dance routine with her own shadow. I am cast as Scarlet's shadow.

After every rehearsal, I enter the green room to find a chorus of critics eager to explain all the ways in which I hadn't quite measured up.

"Ohmigod, good job! Except, you know when Scarlet does that great step-step-kick thing?" chirps one of the Bs. "Your kick kind of looks like . . . like a—"

"Like a turkey," proclaims Roberto, the handsome male

lead, as he runs a hand through his lustrous Italian locks.

"Nah, it's just *stiff*. Hannah's like a robot, and Scarlet's more like a mermaid."

I slam down my collapsible top hat and grit my teeth. "Mermaids can't *kick.*"

"Ugh, sneakers are for homeless people," Cashmere moans at the lunch table one day. "I mean, there's no reason you can't be sporty *and* fashionable." She gestures to her adorably sleek Pumas.

I was laughed out of the dining hall early on for showing brand-name ignorance, so I've taken to laying low and making lots of mental notes: Kenneth Cole, BCBG, Kate Spade, Hermes. Urban Outfitter is trendy, but if you're clad in it from head to toe, you're a poser. The Gap is more than acceptable for basic khakis and plain shirts, but wearing it more than three times a week means you have no fashion imagination. True Religion jeans are the holy grail of denim. Thrift stores are worthless unless you can find something "vintage."

"But doesn't vintage just mean old?"

"No, *Tacky* Friedman. Vintage is, like, *vintage.*"

" . . . Oh."

I beg my mother to take me to the fancy mall across the county, because my wardrobe is in dire need of some updating. She begrudgingly agrees to buy me some new outfits on the condition that I help her scrape out the poop from the bottom of the monkey cage, which tends to get especially crusty come autumn. At Abercrombie, I find some flared corduroys and some shirts featuring the cute embroidered moose logo that are not completely unaffordable. While we're waiting in line, Mom starts browsing through one of the thick catalogues they have stacked near the cash register. Inside, muscular guys with rippling abs and pale waify women frolic in windswept meadows and play rugby and decorate Christmas trees without shirts on. Sometimes without pants, either.

Mom flips through with a quizzical look. "How the hell do they expect to sell clothes when nobody's wearing any?"

A cute guy in a collared shirt with a handful of hangers appears behind us, looking exasperated. "Excuse me, ma'am, but you're going to have to put that down."

"Huh?"

"You have to put the catalogue down. You can't read it in here."

"What do you mean I can't read this in here? It's *your* catalogue."

"The content is not intended for minors."

"All right then." Mom turns the catalogue away from me and continues to read as we move up in the line.

The guy puts down the hangers on a nearby table and crosses his arms. "Ma'am, if you won't put down that catalogue, I'm going to have to ask you to leave."

"I'm about to pay for my daughter's clothes. I don't think you want me to leave."

"I don't think you want me to call security."

The corners of Mom's mouth lift ever so slightly. This kid is challenging her, and she's very amused. She purposefully ignores him and continues to read, this time with a running commentary. "Ooh! Mmm. Oh, that one's got a very nice—"

"Ma'am, I've had about enough."

Mom licks her finger and flips to the next page.

"Mom, seriously, just put it down," I hiss urgently.

A few customers have begun to take notice of the discussion.

"I'm about to give this store my hard-earned money. The least they can do is have the decency not to *harass* me while I'm waiting to do that," she says.

"That's it. I'm calling security."

I lean in. "Mom, cut it out! This is embarrassing!"

"No, you know what's embarrassing?" Mom announces to the entire store. She has an audience now, and she knows it. It's too much for her to resist. "What's really embarrassing is a store that charges exorbitant prices for crappy, unimaginative clothing sewn by malnourished *sweatshop children.*"

We never do get to the front of that line.

On subsequent shopping trips I get blonde highlights and black pumps, which meet with generally positive acclaim. The reviews of my last several English and history papers, however, have not been quite so positive. Apparently, I still have quite a lot to learn. Every assignment comes back ravaged by red pen. It seems that somehow I've even managed to screw up writing my own name. My English teacher, Ms. Lynn, makes a genuine effort to impart the principles of good writing. She thoroughly details the rules of proper outline format and proper footnote format and proper thesis format, but some of the rules are so bizarre that I can't help but raise a hand. Or an eyebrow.

"So, I'm supposed to write what I know, but I can't say the word 'I?'"

"Correct."

"And you want me to prove my point, but I can't use the word 'my'?"

"That's right. No 'my'."

"Okay, I think I've got it. So if I were to write, 'Salinger's symbolic treatment of the hunting hat encourages you to—'"

"No."

I stare at her. Clearly she's joking.

She sighs. "You also can't say 'you'."

"But I'm talking to you!"

A couple of kids around the table groan. It's like I'm stuck in some ridiculous Abbott and Costello routine, and I'm about to make the comparison when I realize that even Ms. Lynn's patience is wearing thin. All this 'I-me-you' stuff aside, she's one of my favorite teachers. She doesn't talk down to us or load us up with busywork, and even though she's tough with a red pen, she is encouraging and she makes me want to work hard. I feel bad for being so combative about these stupid thesis papers.

"Never mind. I get it."

After class, the kid in the oversized green jacket clears his throat and shuffles over to me. "One can understand how one might have been confused," he says in a gravelly bass.

I laugh.

"I'm Mac."

"Ever so pleased to meet one."

He laughs. "School is such bullshit."

We are fast friends.

I imagine Mac was born smoking a pipe and watching a Civil War documentary. His knowledge of history is expansive and almost as eclectic as the contents of his trademark green anorak, which at any one time might include pipe tobacco, underlined copies of *Catch-22* and *Heart of Darkness*, homework from middle school, balls of string, a pocket U.S. Constitution, and melted saltwater taffy. Teachers generally assume he's not paying attention because he never raises his hand, but if put on the spot, Mac can spend half an hour detailing the decline of the Roman Empire as catalyzed by everything from decaying infrastructure and economic instability to the invention of the horseshoe. He'll quote texts that even the teacher hasn't heard of, and halfway through his impassioned impromptu speech he'll pound on the table and proclaim, "Nobiscum Deus!" before finally concluding that no single theory is entirely suitable because they are all too damned reductive, dammit.

I'm studying when Dad knocks on my bedroom door. "Honey, you know how I've been wondering why Danforth doesn't have a rock group?"

"I'm kinda busy, Dad."

"Oh, okay. Well, I ran into the head of the music department today—"

"Mmm hmm," I tell him, not really paying attention.

"Can I come in?"

Damn. "Fine."

He comes in smiling, rocking back and forth on his heels and then twisting side to side with his hands on his hips. He grins. He whistles. He is the most obnoxious thing ever to enter my room in the history of the world. "What is it?" I ask, exasperated.

"Guess."

"Dad, I have homework to do!"

"Oh." He twiddles his thumbs, completely oblivious to my mounting frustration.

"So, what is it?"

"Hmm . . . " He scratches his beard absentmindedly. "Well, uh, the department head said she thought that a band might be a great idea! She said it could give kids the opportunity to, um, hone their chops."

"Great, Dad."

"I know!"

"I really do have a ton of homework though, so—"

"We're going to have so much fun!" He bounds giddily toward the door.

"Wait, *what*? What do you mean, *we*?"

"We're having auditions on Thursday. But don't worry. Somehow," he winks at me from down the hall, "I think you'll make it."

I follow him into the kitchen and glare incredulously at my mother. She shrugs with her hands in the air, palms up, as if to say, 'What do you want me to do?'

Dad is pleased as punch. "First, I figure we can focus on jamming, and then we'll work on really getting into a tight ensemble thing, you know? Is there anything else you think might be fun or helpful?"

It would be helpful if you had just gone ahead and named me Vagina Friedman so I'd be used to the humiliation by now.

If Dad hadn't just spent half his weekend helping me with a poster on the feudal system, I would probably scream. Instead I resolve to take the more adult approach of simply sabotaging the auditions. No auditions, no rock band. No rock band means no fighting, no problems. It's brilliant. My optimism is short-lived, however, because my first step back toward my room lands in a cold, stinky pile of monkey poop. *Shit.*

The week before auditions I tear down all the posters and "forget" to turn in a Morning Meeting announcement. Despite my best efforts at sabotage, I show up to the dreaded first meeting to find that six upperclassmen boys have made the band—all of them better musicians than me, all of them popular, and all of them totally cute.

"Hi, sweet potato!" Dad beams. "I mean, Hannah."

Kill me kill me kill me now.

I honestly don't know how I get through the first hour of rehearsal without strangling Dad with a guitar cord. He openly criticizes Trevor, who is generally acknowledged as king of the Danforth hippies, telling him he has sloppy rhythm and that "thoughtful silences are more important than mindless speed" in drum solos. He calls me "sweetie" more times than I can count. Everyone has to stop and wait while I try to figure out the bass line. My fingers feel clumsier by the second, and all the boys are staring.

"Never mind. Let's just keep going," I whisper urgently.

"But sweetie, you're so close!"

"Dad, *please.*"

"Well, do you want to sing something then? We can work on the bass line at home, honey bunny."

My life is over.

After rehearsal finally mercifully draws to a close, I am headed out of the room when I hear someone say, "Hey, your dad's a pretty cool guy." I turn to find Adam, a dreamy hippie guitarist a year older than me.

I am almost too stunned to speak. "Huh?"

"I said, cool guy." Adam is almost straight out of the forbidden Abercrombie catalogue. He has long, tousled flaxen hair and chiseled features, dotted with just a hint of farm-boy freckle. He smiles at me, showing off the goofy gap in his front teeth. I am imagining him playing rugby in tight white briefs and a jaunty scarf when Dad comes up behind us.

"C'mon, sweetie, we gotta swing by the grocery store on the way home to pick up some Beano. Mom's making burritos for dinner."

I am mortified. My only comfort is in knowing that at least there's nothing, nothing in the entire world that could possibly be more humiliating than this. The worst has got to be over.

Turns out I'm wrong.

A few days later I'm passing the Dell, a cluster of couches set into a giant window box near the basement lockers—one of Danforth's most exclusive hangouts. You can always find mango peels, hacky sacks, and paintbrushes in the Dell, along with all of the coolest upperclassman hippies. Its inhabitants smoke weed and skip class and play guitar. They're too cool to even give Cashmere the time of day. That's why I'm so surprised to hear someone call my name.

"Hannah?"

They must have meant Heather.

"Hannah Banana?"

It's Trevor, king of the hippies. He's idly twirling a set of drumsticks. A scruffy chestnut beard frames his mischievous smile. "Yo, little lady, what's shakin'?"

"Great! I mean—nothing, you?"

"You know, just chillin'. How's that bass line comin'?"

"Oh . . . good, thanks."

Ian, the junior class president, smiles at me from underneath a cacophony of curls. "Hey, you're that chick who got all the funding for the Outdoors club in the student government meeting."

Trevor reaches out to give me a high five. "Yo, that was you? Nice one."

Adam shifts a tall stack of black and white photographs from the couch onto the floor. "Take a load off." He smiles at me. I sneeze loudly, trumpeting like an elephant. *Idiot.*

"Bless you."

"Sorry. Allergies." *Shutupshutup! Cool people don't talk about allergies!*

"It's cool," says a guy in checkered Vans. "My boy Trevor here was so doped up on Robitussin this weekend he crashed his Benz into the country club trying to do donuts in the parking lot."

"Dude, it was only the *gate*, not, like, the clubhouse or something."

"Either way, man, you were fucked up."

"This is true."

"Wow," I say. "Did your parents freak?"

"Nah, I blamed it on the valet."

"Dude, don't be that guy," Ian says, nudging Trevor with his bare foot and shaking his head in disappointment.

"Did he get fired?" I ask.

Trevor folds his arms and kicks his feet up onto the table in front of him, sighing heavily. "Who knows, man. I mean, they all look the same."

The hippies groan and someone chucks a handful of trail mix in Trevor's direction. He ducks, swatting at flying raisins. "Hey, hey! I was kidding! C'mon, I was kidding. You're gonna make me look like a jerk in front of our guest," he says, putting his arm around me protectively.

The guy in the Vans laughs. "What do you think, Hannah? Is this guy a jerk?"

I pause for a moment (*what would Scarlet do?*), and lean back, surveying the group around me with my best scientific face. I fold my arms, sigh dramatically, and declare, "You know, it's really hard to tell . . . I mean, you guys all look the same."

Everyone bursts out laughing. I feel like the funniest girl in the world.

And, just like that, I start getting invitations to sit in the Dell—unheard of for a freshman. The hippies fascinate me because, despite their common love of weed and hatred for "The Man" in all his forms, they're really very diverse. Hippie queen Luna McClane is the daughter of vegan artists who make sculptures and do yoga and write poems about feminine mystique. Trevor is what Adam likes to call a "Trustifarian." Disheveled in a very conspicuously 'check out how totally disheveled I am' sort of way, these trust fund babies blast reggae in their brand-new Audis and then stumble out wearing rumpled vintage T-shirts and dirty jeans, looking like they've just slept on a park bench. They joke about all the holes in their grungy sneakers while making plans to go to their beach houses in Nantucket next weekend.

Adam and Ian, I discover, are of the rebel hippie breed—kids whose parents are super strict, whose every guitar strum and joint toke is a purposeful mutiny against whatever *-ism* is chafing them at the moment—Republicanism, Mormonism, CountryClubism. Adam reads Marx and quotes Marley, and once I think he winked at me during practice. He's dreamy.

I am approaching the Dell before yet another band practice to retrieve the music binder I lent Adam, who's absent today. Just as I turn the corner, I hear Trevor's voice echoing loudly off the metal lockers. "I'm fucking done with it. That guy is a drag. He's like an overweight has-been who—"

I feel hot and embarrassed as I turn to retreat, but I slip on a backpack strap and slam my elbow into a locker, which clatters noisily in protest. Everyone turns.

"Oh," Trevor says, looking uncharacteristically sheepish. "I was just—"

I want to tell Trevor that Dad is right, that his rhythms *are* sloppy, that it *is* important to learn the classics, and that he'll never be prolific if he doesn't get over his own stupid ego. Instead I just swallow hard and shrug. "No, don't worry about it. Rehearsal sucks."

"Yeah. But, like, no disrespect or anything."

"I know."

"Hey, you wanna come blaze with us down by the river?"

"Ah, no, I gotta go—he's expecting me."

"Bummer."

I shrug with deliberate nonchalance. "Whatever."

Out of nowhere, Scarlet comes pirouetting into the center of the Dell and wraps her arms around Trevor's neck. He's her latest object of flirtation. "Hey, cutie, we ready to stock up?"

Scarlet notices me. "Oh, hey, it's the shadow girl! Are you coming, too?"

Some of the Dell guys turn to look at me.

"Um, nah, I gotta do this rehearsal thing."

"You have to come! You can't just leave me alone with all these dirty *boys*! Come on, we'll only be gone for like twenty minutes," Scarlet says, taking my hands in hers.

Before I know it, I'm in Trevor's Audi. He blasts Zeppelin. As we pull out, I slump down into the seat to make sure nobody sees me breaking the rules by leaving campus in another student's car. Nobody else seems concerned. We drive down the hill and pull up behind an old factory by the river. Trevor removes a joint from his shirt pocket and lights up. He takes a long drag and passes it to me.

I try my best to reply with an I-smoke-drugs-all-the-time-but-just-don't-feel-like-it-right-now "No thanks," instead of an ohmigod-ohmigod-we're-going-to-get-arrested "No thanks," but it comes out as more of a mumble.

A shady-looking kid wearing dark sunglasses pulls up in a beat-up sedan with the speakers blaring. Everyone piles out of Trevor's car. I follow nervously.

Scarlet passes the kid a thick wad of bills, which he counts carefully. He grabs a rolled-up Ziploc baggie out of his backpack and hands it to her. *Ohmigod you're at a drug deal. What the hell are you doing at a drug deal? Isn't this the part in the movie where someone gets shot? What if it's a setup?!*

Scarlet unrolls the bag and looks inside, then whispers something to Trevor, who squints, shakes his head, and gestures toward the car.

"What's that, Shorty?" the shady kid wants to know.

"Oh, I was just telling him that I know you're not trying to short me, because I know you would never want to lose one of your most beautiful, loyal customers."

He pauses. "Right."

Smiling like a beauty queen, she walks right up to him and gives him a very light kiss on the cheek. "Thanks, handsome," she croons, and then shoos us back into Trevor's car. The kid stands there, looking confused.

Trevor starts up the car. "What the hell was that? He totally tried to rip you off. You want me to—"

Scarlet motions for him to wait, and right on cue, the kid appears at the passenger window. She rolls it down and he hands her another little baggie. "That other bag was for another customer. This should make it even."

"Thanks. You're a doll," she says, blowing him a kiss as she rolls up the window.

Trevor is dumbstruck. "How did you—"

"Always leave them wanting more," she explains with a satisfied smile.

Suddenly, we see flashing lights coming across the bridge.

"Oh, shit," Trevor says, shifting into gear and speeding around to the far side of the factory, where he pulls in behind a tall stack of old wooden crates and waits. "Is he gone?"

My heart is racing as Trevor rolls down the windows to air out the car. "Shouldn't we get out of here?" I ask, trying to suppress the panic in my voice as I realize that our options are either getting caught by the police with an intoxicated driver, or else having that intoxicated driver attempt a quick getaway.

We stay hidden behind the crates, hearts pounding, until Trevor is sure that the cop car is gone, but I'm still terrified that Trevor is too high to drive. I make an excuse about having to pick up something in town, and I walk the entire way back to school all alone, certain that I've ruined my chances at coolness forever.

By the time I arrive, I'm a full forty minutes late for rehearsal. I find my dad sitting dutifully in the music room, noodling around on a guitar, also all alone. It's pathetic.

"Hi, sweetie! Is everything all right?"

"Where is everybody?"

"Oh. Well, I thought you might know."

"No, I—I had to stay late with a teacher."

"That's okay. Maybe the other kids had to, too."

"Yeah, maybe."

I know I should be happy that everyone bailed. It could very well mean the death of the extracurricular from hell. I've been praying for something like this. But as Dad checks his watch for the eighth time in five minutes, somehow I don't feel as relieved as I thought I would.

"Honey, would you mind passing out these jazz charts? That way we can hit the ground running when everybody gets here." I help him distribute the charts he spent all night making onto six empty music stands that I know will not be filled.

"I'm sure this is just a busy week," Dad explains thoughtfully.

"Yeah, probably," I tell him.

When nobody shows up for another half-hour, we collect

the music and pack it back into the car. I don't know if I'm angrier at Trevor for being so cocky and making fun of my dad, or at Dad for being such an easy target, for being so boring and lame. I hate him. I don't want to be anything like him. No wonder I was such a loser before. It's in my goddamn DNA.

But you don't have to be stuck the way that you were born. Scarlet says that's what hair dye is for.

When Cashmere invites me for an outing at the fanciest mall outside of New York City, I am thrilled to have the opportunity to observe fashion etiquette firsthand. I try on four different outfits before settling on one that seems trendy without looking like I was *trying* to seem trendy—dark bellbottoms from Camden Market with little orange flames embroidered on the bell, a paisley cotton top, a colorful beaded necklace, and a reddish floor-length trench coat my mom got in college.

I meet up with Dot and Cashmere, who both wear crisp collared shirts, designer jeans, and diamond earrings. I wonder how the hell I managed to be both over- and underdressed at the same time.

Cashmere waves and smiles.

"Anne! So wonderful to see you!" Dot gushes.

"Her name is Hannah, Mother."

"Nonsense, darling, she's—"

"It actually *is* Hannah."

"And don't you look *adorable* in that little coat. It's darling! Did you make it yourself?"

"No, it's my mom's from college."

"How absolutely adorable. Well, girls: shall we?"

We shop.

Dot waxes poetic about the respective merits of Burberry and Armani while Cashmere and I discuss school.

"Ugh, wasn't Friday's Spanish test *brutal*?" I moan.

"I know! She didn't even *mention* irregular subjunctive, and then half the questions—"

"I still don't know why you didn't choose French." Dot interjects. "Just imagine, you could be ordering for us at Le Cinq this summer instead of sorting out Lupita's green card crisis. But don't worry about the tests, darling, it's not like the immigrants know anything about proper grammar."

Cashmere closes her eyes and smoothes her hair.

We enter the Mecca of makeup—every corner and countertop is lined with crèmes, powders, and polishes of every possible shade. Cashmere picks out a vial of cranberry lip gloss, which Dot replaces with an "attractive yet tasteful" clear version because "cranberry is for girls in leather miniskirts." Dot taps her foot impatiently at the makeup counter while waiting for someone to bring her the limited edition moisturizer made from special sea parsley and essence of narcissus, which is so expensive that it is kept under a double lock; two separate keys are required to access it, much like the launch codes on a nuclear missile sub.

"Sweetie!" I hear someone exclaim as a stick-thin pair of arms encircles my waist. It's Teagan. "Ohmigod, I can't believe you're here, *too*! Me and the girls are going upstairs to check out the new Betsey Johnson. You guys, like, totally have to come!"

Cashmere glances toward her mother, who is busy accusing a saleswoman of being intentionally incompetent. "Yeah—yeah, let's do it. Mom? Mom, can I meet you back here after Tea and Hannz and I check out the new—"

Dot's head whips around. "Are you *sure*, dear? Because we have a lot of—"

"Yeah, Mom, I'm sure."

"Aha. Very well, then. I want you back here in forty-five minutes and not a minute more. I have to—"

She's still talking as we disappear into an adjacent aisle and make for the escalator.

Teagan clasps her hands dramatically and presses her nose into a glass display case. "I think I'm in love."

Cashmere comes over to inspect the sunglasses. "Ooh, the tortoiseshell? They're perfect."

"I know, right?"

"You should get them."

"I need them."

"You totally need them. What do you think, Hannz?"

"They're cute," I say, willing myself not to gasp when I see the sticker: $650.

Price tags give me the creeps. They always have. Dad never pays any attention to them, and Mom pays way too much attention to them. The inevitable conflicts that follow make me think of the men in black suits, with their little notepads and lots of questions, of tight budgets and broken transmissions and tense passive-aggressive whispering in the back of a bus that smells of wet dog.

Even though I seldom volunteer to do the dishes, I have become an expert grocery packer in order to avoid seeing Mom make the super-depressing "we can't afford this" face at the cash register. If you squeeze past the cart and concentrate really hard on double bagging and putting cans on the bottom and making sure the produce doesn't get squashed, you can usually miss the entire exchange. Unless, of course, the cashier says the total out loud, in which case it doesn't matter if you can't see Mom's face because you can imagine it, and that's even worse.

For this reason, I have always regarded cash registers as untrustworthy automated frown boxes. Even if I know I have enough money to afford something I need, the back of my brain still feels a little tight and overheated just before the total is rung up.

Teagan, however, does not seem to suffer from any such affliction. She swipes her credit card with glee and, like magic, the glasses disappear from the case, only to reappear seconds later on her face. She skips around the mall for a while, turning to us every so often to make a quick kissyface before stopping to inspect her reflection in a store window. She frowns and sticks out her tongue. "Blech," she says. "They make my nose look fat."

"Not true," Cashmere tells her.

Without another word, Teagan removes the offending glasses and deposits them into her handbag *du jour*, never to be seen again.

I follow the girls into Coach and bebe and Gucci, watching in awe as they amass armfuls of merchandise, talking about all the must-haves that I never even knew existed—dusters, clutches, wraps, and more.

Teagan and Cashmere take over whole blocks of dressing rooms in order to try things on. We critique. If an outfit gets a resounding "Cute!" then it's rung up immediately, but anything thought to be "tacky" or "cheap" gets the boot. I try things on too, playing dress up in all sorts of outfits that I never intend to buy before zipping myself into a stunning floor-length black gown.

"Ah, the Badgley Mischka! That's *perfect* on you," a saleswoman coos.

The delicately draped black lace is cut with a high halter neck and pulls up my nearly nonexistent boobs, while the empire waist gives me a smooth, hourglass figure. No wonder everyone's gaga for designer dresses—this fits like a dream. It *is* perfect.

"Can I ring it up?"

It is also, like, three thousand dollars. *Sure*, I imagine telling her, *just give me a minute to sell my kidney on the black market and I'll meet you at the register.*

"Um, I'm gonna have to think about it, but thank you."

"It's *really* not you, Hannz," Cashmere assures me, shaking her head. "Take it off."

I glance once more at the price tag and realize that she's right. It's not me. I take it off.

Before I have time to protest, I find myself buried underneath a mountain of shopping bags, getting swiveled around on a spindly stool while a flatiron sizzles dangerously close to my scalp.

"This is a frizz intervention," Cashmere declares. "Just watch our bags for a sec. The girls and I have to check out Louis Vuitton."

"Is it supposed to smell like something's burning?" I ask the flamboyant man in tight pants who is leaning over me.

"Shhshshh. Don't worry your frizzy little head, child," he says.

I sit and fiddle with my fingernails until the girls finally return, each toting a bag containing another much more expensive bag.

"Ohmigod, you look, like, fierce! For serious," squeals Teagan.

All the Bs nod their heads approvingly.

The man in the tight pants finishes his work with a flourish, swiveling me around to face the mirror. I almost don't recognize myself. My hair looks like magazine hair. It shines. I run my fingers through the silky locks without them snagging on a massive tangle of curls. The strands part like water. Stranger still, framed by my shiny new pin-straight hairdo, my face seems different—stronger, sleeker, more professional.

"This is the best deal on ceramic plates you're ever gonna find," the man in the tight pants tells me cheerily. "They're treated with moisturizing ions and nanoparticles and you can take one home for only $149!"

"Wow, well, thank you so much, but I'll have to think about it."

"We'll take one," Dot announces, appearing from the other side of the cart, putting her arm around Cashmere, and passing the man a credit card. Platinum.

Later that night, Cashmere is reviewing her purchases while I wait for my mother to come pick me up. "These are going to be perfect for the freshman fashion show. I'm so excited that you brought it back! You're the best, Hannz."

Just as I'm about to leave, Cashmere stops me at the door. "Oh, and one more thing . . ." She slips a slim, rectangular package out of her purse and passes it to me. It's another flat-iron, just like the one her mom bought.

"But how—"

She smiles deviously and shrugs. "Guess it just fell in. See you in school, gorgeous. Kisses!"

For my next several assignments, I extract every ounce of humor, relevance, and original thought and stick to the simplest possible format. Strict outline, cold hard facts. When they are returned, the only comments written in red are big fat A's.

I. This month I have:

    A. Managed to tailor my motions to match Scarlet's almost exactly.

    B. Received three hugs from Roberto in the green room.

    C. Mastered the art of hair straightening.

II. This month I've also learned to:

    A. Spot a knockoff Louis Vuitton purse a Chinatown block away.

    B. Detect the subtle razors of tension underlying all Great Eight conversations, e.g.:

        a. "That sweater is gorgeous, it totally draws attention from your hips."

        b. "Ohmigod, you look so nice today! I almost didn't recognize you!"

        c. "That's what I love about you, Tea. You make me feel so smart."

    C. Eat raw fish without getting squeamish. Sushi!

III. Still have to pinch myself to believe that I'm:

    A. In the Great Eight.

    B. On the Dean's List.

    C. No longer a Freak.

chapter seven

POPULARITY SUCKS

I have just ruined a three-hundred-dollar jar of caviar.

Apparently, you are not supposed to dip the tiny pancake into the fish eggs like they're guacamole. I realize this too late, only after Cashmere's father furrows his brow ever so slightly at the creamy white trail squiggling its way between the little black orbs. Dot takes a long swig of her martini. Her third. Silence. I fight to swallow without betraying the caviar's salty assault on my tongue, but I can't escape the thought of a thousand itty bitty infant fish shrieking as I gulp the whole thing down. Should I scoop that white stuff out? Why isn't anybody talking? And how is this black goo worth three hundred dollars an ounce? I long for the boisterous bagels-and-lox of my youth as the four of us sit in the formal dining room listening to the snow fall outside.

Suddenly, Dot bursts out laughing. Hysterically. Nobody else even looks up, but she continues to cackle, so I ask, "What's so funny, Mrs. Wescott?"

"Oh, nothing." She runs her fingers along the jumbo pearls

adorning her neck. "I was just remembering a long time ago when Richard said something particularly witty. You remember, Richard? Back when you were thin?"

Richard places his wine glass on the table and leaves.

More silence.

"You forgot to use a coaster!" Dot shrieks, tilting her martini glass back all the way.

Over the past semester I have discovered that getting ready is never a one-person job. Before any major social function, it's customary, nay *mandatory*, to call up your friends and ask the all–important question: "What are you wearing?" No one person is ever the final authority on whether a concert calls for simple jeans and T-shirts or is worthy of Miu Miu miniskirts and ornate Nanette Lepore tops, but somehow, after three or four "What are you wearing?" phone calls, everyone usually shows up looking exactly the same. Except for me, of course. I usually show up looking like the Etch-a-Sketch version of whatever classic designer vision the girls have conjured. Still, it's important to coordinate. You don't want to show up in jeans at some fancy parent-hosted cocktail hour. It's even worse to arrive dressed to the nines at a party that's casual. You'll seem desperate.

Tonight is anything but casual. The Holiday Ball is the fanciest school function of the year, and it's taking place at Rosewood Palace. Everything has to be perfect.

Cashmere noted my lack of eye contouring a few weeks ago as her chauffeured car drove us back to her house to do math homework. When I stabbed myself in the eye with the charcoal liner she handed me, she declared an intervention.

"You're coming over before Holiday Ball," she said. "This is a fashion emergency."

Cashmere is smooth and careful as she mixes moisturizers with light face tint, applying the combination with delicate dabs. "Ta-da! No more patchy red cheeks." She powders my face, blends along my jaw line, de-oils my T-zone, highlights my inner lower lids, and shades the apples of my cheeks. I never knew my face had so many different places on it.

"You look good," she says of the crushed red velvet dress my aunt had given me from one of her many stints as a bridesmaid. "But it needs something . . . "

She disappears and comes back holding black pointy witch shoes. "Hannz, meet Jimmy Choo."

"Are those the ones your mom wore on your birthday?"

Cashmere looks at me like I'm nuts. "Eiw, those ones were like, ancient. *These* aren't even out till next season. I borrowed 'em last week from Teagan; her mom knows someone at Vogue. They're going to be *perfect.*"

I slide my feet into the shiny patent leather and wonder what it was my mother and I had hated so much about pointy-toed heels all those months ago.

"One more thing," Cashmere announces. "You need a signature scent—something people will remember you for. I got mine in France, but you can use my old one if you want." She sprays a perfumed cloud into the air and has me walk through it. "First we mist, then we dab behind the ear. That way, if you lean in close, the guy will remember you."

A silver bell chimes. "Ah, that means my hair's done. Help me get the rollers out?" I wait as Cashmere expertly applies her makeup, pulls on nude stockings, then disappears into her closet. When she emerges, she is radiant. She twirls. She's wearing the black Badgley Mischka.

"You like?"

"I like."

You. bitch.

We stand in front of the mirror together just before the limousine arrives to take us to the ball, and I find it impossible to stay mad at Cashmere after seeing the makeover she's given me. For as long as I can remember, I've wished I were some sort of princess. And for the first time in my life, I actually look the part.

Rosewood Palace is decked out for the holidays. An enormous Christmas tree with delicate silver ornaments stands sparkling in the corner, candles and colored lights fill the ballroom with a sweet cheery glow, and evergreen garlands weave up the grand, sweeping staircase. It's like a holiday fairy tale.

"Hey, shadow girl, when'd you get so sexy?" It's Scarlet, looking stunning as usual, towering over me in floor-length red Dior. She's been bragging about this outfit for a month. She gracefully descends the princess staircase, flanked by four female groupies, plus Roberto, upon whom she drapes herself because her college boyfriend couldn't make it. Roberto runs his fingers through his trademark long hair, looks up at me, and does a double take. "Wow," he says.

The music changes. It's a fast song. Scarlet claps her hands and dashes off toward the DJ booth with her entourage in tow.

Roberto extends his hand. "Care to dance, shadow girl?"

Oh. My. God. Play it cool. I tilt my head. "I thought I danced like a turkey," I remind him.

"Well, you don't *look* like a turkey," he smiles.

What would Scarlet do? "And you don't look like a jerk," I hear myself say. I freeze awkwardly, waiting to see how this joke has landed. Maybe it's only okay when Scarlet does that.

Roberto nods with a wry smirk. "Touché, shadow girl."

Yes. I take a step toward him, run my fingers along his shoulder like I've seen Scarlet do so many times, lean in and whisper, "It's *Hannah*," and then walk away, my new/old signature scent lingering coyly in his nostrils.

The shock of the suaveness of this move compels me to go out onto the veranda to get some fresh air. *Holy* crap! *Did I really just do that? Who was that person?* I am reminded of my awkward self as soon as I reach the last marble step, which is covered in a thin layer of ice that sends me flying straight into a frost-covered decorative topiary. *Idiot.* I recover and pick some damp leaves out of my hair before noticing a cloud of blonde curls bobbing up the hillside toward the palace.

"Ian!" I shout out to the dandelion puff. He's dressed like a mountaineer and grinning mighty wide. He jogs up to meet me.

"What are you doing here?" I ask.

"We came for refreshments," he giggles, gesturing to a ragtag band of hippies emerging from the far woods. "Hey," he twirls me once by the hand, "has anyone told you lately that you're as lovely as a peach blossom on a summer afternoon?"

"Way to lay low, jackoff!" I hear Trevor shout from the darkness. "Why not just blaze in the middle of the fucking dance floor?"

"Chill out, man. She's cool," says Ian, jogging up the palace steps and disappearing inside.

"Oh, it's Hannah Banana!" Trevor saunters over and throws his arm around me playfully.

Luna complains about how the mass-produced bubblegum pop playing in the ballroom will be the downfall of civilized society while Trevor rolls his eyes. Dreamy Adam with the farm-boy freckles doesn't say too much, but as I'm leaving to return to the ball I think he winks at me. No, I'm sure of it.

I pass through a long receiving line of teachers and administrators in the palace foyer, coming in just as Ian is leaving again. He hugs me, a task made substantially more difficult by the fact that he's now balancing a huge silver platter of miniature éclairs on each hand. He smiles and nods politely at several scowling administrators, nonchalantly squeezing his way past them and out the door, whistling all the while. His blonde curls bounce down the steps and disappear into the night.

I'm about to join the girls back at the party when I notice a huge scratch across the side of my left Jimmy Choo shoe, no doubt the result of my pratfall a little earlier. *Shit.* Shitshitshit. Teagan and Cashmere have shoe radar; they'll notice immediately. I have to fix it. I sneak through the kitchen and into the study, where I desperately search for a black ink pen in the massive oak desk.

"Trying to slit your wrists with a letter opener?" Julian asks, appearing in the doorway in a tux and Sinatra fedora, swaying a little tipsily. "I know this debutante scene is a drag, toots, but you shouldn't give them the satisfaction of knowing they got to you. Liquor's quicker."

"Nobody *got* to me. I'm just looking for a pen," I say.

"This kind of pen?" he poses, holding out a Sharpie.

"Where'd you find that?"

"Man's gotta have his secrets." He ambles over and looms

curiously as I grab the pen and desperately fill in the scratch with ink.

"Does your whole snazzy get-up disappear at midnight or something?"

"*Please*, Julian, just leave me alone."

"As long as you promise to call me before you start drawing your dress back on."

"Fuck off."

"Sorry. Bad Julian, bad," he says, smacking his cheeks playfully as he strolls out of the room.

The touch-up job is surprisingly effective.

I dance in a tight circle with the rest of the Great Eight until I have to catch the midnight train home. I watch how Cashmere gracefully sways her hips, and I peer across the room at Scarlet just as Roberto leads her in a long dramatic dip down to the floor. At a quarter to midnight, I'm on my way out the door when Teagan confronts me in the foyer.

"Um, are those, like, *my* shoes?"

"Cashmere lent them to me. Sorry, I didn't—"

"'Cuz that's, like, totally cool and everything, but I, like, need them for a benefit tomorrow, so . . . " She holds out her hand expectantly.

"But I have to walk to the train station," I say softly.

"Bummer."

I don't feel bad about the scuff anymore. I get a ride from Dot down to the train station, where a pair of black tuxedo legs dangles from the roof of the platform awning. I fiddle in my purse. "Hey, I have your pen," I shout to the ceiling, shivering.

Julian swings down from the precarious ledge with a stumble and a cigarette in his mouth. He looks me over. "Guess your fairy godmother wasn't so generous, eh?" he says, pointing at my stocking feet.

I hand him the pen.

"Look at you. You're shivering." He takes off his jacket and sweeps it gallantly around my shoulders.

"Thanks."

He reaches to pull his silver flask from inside the jacket, offering it to me.

"No, thanks."

We wait in the cold for many minutes before the tracks start to rattle. The wind whips quickly across the platform as the train pulls in with a roar.

"Did you use that pen on your eyes, too?" Julian asks, extending a hand to help me as we step onto the train. "Because, for the record, you're the prettiest raccoon I have ever lent my jacket to."

The day before finals I'm sitting with Cashmere and the rest of the girls when I look around the lunchroom and I see it: cliques have formed. There's a table of boisterous jocks, some popped-collar preppies, the Chinese kids who miss their parents and never speak English, the geeks, the goths, the girls with long hair who don't wear bras, the guys with the long hair who don't kiss girls, and then there's us. We are the Park Place of freshman lunch table real estate.

I can't freakin' believe it.

In one electrifying moment, I realize that I am actually popular. This is the high school equivalent of discovering that you are, in fact, the head of Microsoft and the Queen of England combined in the body of a Victoria's Secret model, this after many years of being about as well-loved as a deadly communicable disease. From Black Plague to White American Princess—not too shabby. I savor the moment, twirling a strand of my stick-straight hair between my fingers and licking my glossy lips with satisfaction. I, Hannah Friedman, am sitting at the popular table. And they don't even want my answers to last night's homework.

chapter eight

INSECURITY SUCKS

When Scarlet returns for her senior year thirty pounds lighter than her already lovely frame, the rumor mill churns out speculations faster than they can be debunked.

"Anorexic. Definitely anorexic," a Great Eighter declares.

"No! She went to a macrobiotic meditation retreat in Tibet and now she only eats raw organic vegan food," says one of the Bs.

"Fish sticks aren't vegan, retard."

"Fine, raw organic *pescetarian* food," the B corrects, flipping her hair.

"And I heard she chugs, like, apple cider vinegar, and has, like, totally detoxified her body from the ravages of modern pollutants," Teagan says. We all turn to look at her in surprise. "What?" she asks, blushing at all the attention. "It's this month's *Cosmo* cover."

"But what about all the cigarettes?" Cashmere asks. "They're pretty toxic."

Teagan shrugs. "I don't know, doesn't tobacco come from

plants? Maybe she smokes organic. Whatever it is, she looks like a fucking supermodel."

The girls in Scarlet's dorm determine that the key ingredients in the supermodel recipe are dieting, purging, and cocaine. The thinner Scarlet gets, the more of an idol she becomes, and many begin to regard calorie counting as the path to enlightenment. I am enraptured by the way silver Tiffany bangles hang loosely on her thin wrists, the way her cheekbones carve a permanent, sexy pout into once-chubby adolescent cheeks. I am enthralled by her ever-increasing wardrobe of size-0 Versace suede slacks and hand-beaded silk blouses that billow gracefully where her breasts used to be.

That she now swathes herself in thick pashminas, even on oppressively hot days, simply seems part of her new persona. Though we notice that she can no longer hit the high notes in choir, that her witty comebacks are frequently delayed as she searches for words, and that a downy white fuzz has begun to creep down her neck and colonize her collarbones, no one thinks anything of it. It comes with the territory. She is fiery yet frail, a delicate princess with as much of a proclivity for ranting as fainting, in either case garnering much more attention in two minutes than I have managed to amass in my entire high school career. The boys worship her.

In dance class, I choose the locker opposite hers in an attempt to observe and hopefully absorb some of her seemingly effortless eminence. I watch as she pokes at her hip bones, which jut out from her black leotard.

"Congratulate me, ladies!" Scarlet chirps, summoning her clique of pretty senior dancers.

"What did Jordan do now—propose?" her best friend gushes.

"No. He's such a *doll*, though. Check out this promise ring: two carats!" She gleefully displays a very shiny rock on her very bony finger. "The news is . . . I reached my low goal! I thought I would never get past 115, but this morning I stepped on the scale, and finally," she pauses for effect, "105!"

A flutter of admiring "ooohs" follows.

Only the plainest member of the clique seems anything less than enthused. "Scarlet, you should really take it easy."

Scarlet scoffs. "What, didn't think I could do it?"

"That's not what I said. It's just—you looked pretty out of it today in math."

"Who *isn't* put to sleep by Donaghy's babbling?" Scarlet snaps back, removing jazz shoes from her locker and slamming it noisily.

The other girls proceed into the dance studio, leaving Scarlet, her best friend, and me alone in the dressing room. Scarlet drapes a matchstick arm around the friend, and I strain to listen without appearing to be listening. "Besides, we know how to fix sleepy," I hear her coo softly as she brushes a beautifully manicured finger along the side of her nose, "but homely is forever." The two nod conspiratorially before they disappear, skipping into the hallway toward the bathroom, giggling like hyenas.

Auditions for the fall musical roll around again, and I am slated to sing after Scarlet, a professionally trained opera singer, and a girl who everyone says is a genuine Japanese pop star taking time off to get her high school diploma. After hearing all of their solos, each one more unbelievable than the last, it's my turn to go. My knees shake and my neck stiffens. My breath is shallow and weak and I can't get the notes out. Everyone's watching. I ask to start over, and the accompanist begrudgingly plays my intro again.

I can feel my body betraying me as it rasps and warbles through the familiar tune I've practiced so many times before. I get nervous and clutch my diaphragm approaching the final high note, which I totally nailed in the shower, on the train, and in the dining hall just before the audition. Each time it rang out clearly with a hint of sweet vibrato as I imagined myself surrounded by backup dancers doing high kicks. This time it comes out like my throat farted. It's horrific. People wince.

My audition for the traveling a cappella choir is even more of a disaster. Some German kid takes my place as first chair saxophone in jazz band, so I stop practicing altogether. I quit piano. I quit guitar. I'm tired of feeling like a musical failure. I'll never live up to Dad's level of musicality, but what has it gotten him anyway? Dangling gutters and no friends and a broken transmission. Well, my life is going to be different.

I think about Scarlet, how everything about her seems to shimmer with star dazzle and pink champagne. *Spring break in Paris! Limited edition Prada! My boyfriend's brand new Porsche!* I want that. I am convinced the confidence that has eluded me my entire life will be mine, if only I can become a little more like her. As I watch my own black leotard galumphing along in the dance class mirror next to hers, I decide to give up cookies and hope for the best.

Over the summer Julian got his driver's license and a brand new Mercedes, so he stops riding the train. I start spending more time with Mac and the oddball upperclassman commuters he has befriended. A motley band of malcontents, they're bonded only by their matching monthly train passes and their inability to fit into the usual cliques. The train gang is truly the bizarre underbelly of Danforth society. There's the kid who sounds like Iago, the parrot from *Aladdin,* and solves quadratic equations in his head, the kid whose parents own the weird little cheese shop down county and always reeks of Gruyère, and the kid in the black trench coat who compulsively clutches a copy of Nietzsche.

We jump between moving train cars and sneak into the conductor's booth to make silly announcements, and we stage elaborate competitions to ease the boredom of the hour-long ride. Trivia contests give way to blackjack and poker, and then one day someone brings in a full *Risk* board game. We balance it across our laps, leading forces through Kamchatka and decimating cavalry in Australia until the train lurches to a halt, littering the aisle with tiny little pieces. Mac takes credit, declaring that he's in cahoots with the conductor and that this is his masterful coup. We can't stop laughing for long enough to set up a new game.

The train guys are just easier than girls. Instead of giving each other fake compliments underscored by years of jealous hostility, their ribbings are upfront and good-natured. The only time they even mention clothing is to tease Mac about his health hazard of a coat, and the only time they ever want gossip is when the warfare at my lunch table becomes a public spectacle.

"Great Eight strikes again?" Mac asks after a particularly stormy lunch leaves most of the Bs in tears. B1 made out with

B2's BF. B3 must now side with whomever she decides is her BFF. I'm busy at the salad bar when the gauntlet is thrown down, but I can hear the screams all the way across the dining hall. Betrayal is in the air.

"Don't even get me started," I tell Mac.

"And you keep going back to them because . . . ?"

"They're my friends."

"Sheesh. Sure would hate to meet your enemies."

If you're not attractive to the opposite sex in high school, you're pretty much social road kill, and I am quickly discovering that it takes even more than designer jeans, lengthening mascara, and juicy gossip to stay ahead of the headlights. The girls tease me mercilessly about my train gang friends to the point where I'm embarrassed to even say hello to them in the hallway. But being in the right clique isn't nearly as important as looking like you belong in it. This year, skirts shorten, heels lengthen, and breasts must be lifted, shaped, and enhanced for every outfit and occasion—strapless bras, pushup bras, padded bras, convertibles, and racer backs. God help you if you're flat.

I'm not so flat anymore. Over the summer, my breasts swelled to fill the whole of my cupped hand, but a lot of other things swelled, too. I was such a cute wispy little thing when I was a kid. Now my cheeks are chubby, my thighs jiggle, and no matter how many sit-ups I do, I can never get rid of the little pooch that sticks out over my jeans. I'm bigger than my mother for the first time in my life, and it's embarrassing. When the family eats dinner together, she sits next to Sam, and I feel like I'm on the chubby side of the table with my dad.

I research. There are a million magazine articles: "Drop 30 Lbs. in a Month," "10 Tips for the Best Bikini Body," "How Mary-Kate Lost the Weight." Anytime I'm in the grocery store, I can spot them from all the way down the aisle—glossy pictures of beautiful women with dramatically contoured collarbones. Their silhouettes are flawless, elegant, and lean. I study their stomachs, so perfectly toned and tanned, and their calves, two slender tapering lines. Mine bulge out roundly like pale cartoon whales.

I try a diet, or to be more precise, a new diet every other week. First it's no sugar, then no carbs, then (inexplicably) no white foods, then only raw foods, and on and on until I'm so adept at calorie counting that I can estimate the grams of fat in an entire meal without a second glance. I lose a few pounds and congratulate myself. It's kind of fun. I'm good at this.

It's Cashmere's birthday again, sweet sixteen, and this year I am invited for pre-party preparation. We are halfway through the snacks and an episode of *The Real World* when Dot pulls me aside, looking absolutely panicked.

"Cashmere needs to see you. *Now.*"

Dot hurries me upstairs to where Cashmere sits cross-legged on the center of her canopy bed, the kind I wasn't allowed to get on account of how much dust they collect. She's wearing a silk robe and clutching a decorative pillow.

"What are they wearing?" she asks anxiously.

"What?"

She smoothes out her robe. "*What* are they *wearing?*"

"The girls? I dunno, skirts and jeans and stuff."

"Jeans?"

" . . . some of them."

"How many of them?"

"Three or four?"

Dot sighs. "I told you."

Cashmere leaps up. "No, I told *you*, Mother. I told you that if we didn't put it on the invitation, they'd do it just to spite me."

Dot gets up and walks straight out the door. She just leaves. Cashmere bursts into tears. *Um . . . is this like a private moment or something? Should I leave, too?*

"Is everything okay?" I ask tentatively.

"They came for the Kate Spade pencil cases, and they wore jeans to spite me, and now they're all down there *laughing* at me."

"They're laughing at MTV!"

"They hate me." She hurls the pillow across the room. "They *hate* me!" She storms over to her closet and throws open the doors, revealing a room the size of my bedroom packed with racks upon racks of clothes and shoes arranged by color, and an entire wall of purses in every imaginable shade. She starts grabbing stilettos and flinging them over her shoulders one by one. "Ugh, I hate these shoes." Cashmere kicks off her slippers and frantically tries on a few pairs before collapsing in a pouty pile of silk.

Just then, Dot returns carrying a huge pink package covered with dozens of tiny, shiny bows. "I was going to save this until after the party, darling, but I thought you could use a little pick-me-up." She hiccups.

"If this is that horrible, dowdy brown pea coat, Mother, I'm going to scream."

Cashmere tears off the wrapping and removes pair after pair after pair of crisp dark blue jeans. Cavalli, Juicy, True Religion, Citizens, Sevens—the crème de la crème of Bloomingdale's denim section. I remember going with my mother this summer to purchase a pair of Sevens, which I had been saving for months to afford.

"$225 for a pair of jeans?!" Mom balked. "For that much money, they better get me off."

"Eiw, Ma, gross."

Cashmere seems mollified and sashays back to the closet with an armful of denim. She shuts the door to try them on.

"SIX?" we hear her scream a minute later. "You bought me size SIX?!" Cashmere bounds out of the closet wearing a new pair of jeans and brandishing the tag of another.

Dot nods. "They fit you marvelously, darling."

"They're *enormous*."

"Well, you were practically *bursting* out of the old ones," Dot responds curtly.

Cashmere's blue eyes blaze. "Out," she growls through gritted teeth, pointing to the door.

"Don't you dare—"

"Just get out. And send them all home," Cashmere demands, pointing downstairs. "Send them *home*. The party is over."

Dot folds her arms. "No party, no presents."

"I don't want your *fucking* presents."

Dot turns to me. "Would you please tell Cashmere that if she doesn't stop being a petulant child, she's not going to get the—"

"I just want you to get *out!*" Cashmere shrieks.

Dot raises her eyebrow defiantly and purses her lips. She

slides her hand into the pocket of her sleek dress pants and retrieves a shiny black object dangling from a silver chain. She jabs her thumb into the middle, hard.

Suddenly, we hear a car alarm blaring from outside.

Cashmere gasps and her eyes widen as she dashes over to the window. I follow, tracking her delighted gaze to a beautiful black car with an extravagant red bow on top.

"BMW!" she shrieks, jumping up and down with excitement.

Dot walks up behind us. "Happy birthday," she says flatly. Then she hurls the keychain right out the window, turns on her heel, and marches straight out the door.

After a tearful key recovery mission and an extensive wardrobe consultation, Cashmere finally selects the perfect outfit. I join the other girls in the formal living room just as the lights are dimmed. Lupita arrives with the cake. Dot gestures grandly to the staircase. There stands Cashmere, pretty as a picture, perfectly poised on the top step. She descends slowly, gracefully, as we sing "Happy Birthday," covering her mouth as if to show embarrassment, as if she never intended for anyone to make such a fuss. Illuminated by the soft glow of the tiny pink candles, Cashmere demurely ponders her birthday wish with closed eyes and an angelic smile.

Dot kisses her on the cheek. They pose for a picture. Cashmere blows out her sixteen candles, and we can't help but clap.

It looks absolutely perfect.

The insular world of Danforth is rocked on the morning of September 11. Everyone gathers in the dining hall to hear what little information is known—by now, two planes have crashed into the World Trade Center towers, which dominate the New York City skyline just upriver. All cell phone service is down, so kids whose parents work in or around the towers dial and redial hysterically. Some kids walk down to the river to see the city burn, while others sprint to the computer lab and start shouting out updates as they trickle in from the news feed. Passenger planes. One in Pennsylvania. Both towers collapse. A full-scale attack.

I'm surprised by how unsurprised I am. The news is horrifying, but it feels like the disaster my mother and my grandmother were always preparing me for. Although I'm pretty sure that Danforth is not too high on the list of terrorist targets, by the time we hear that a plane has crashed into the Pentagon I fully expect to have to arm myself with the sharp end of a protractor and fight my way to the coast so that I can swim to safety. But the day ends and the smoke clears. Life moves on.

For weeks afterward I am addicted to the news footage. I watch transfixed as the planes glide into the buildings like stones breaking the surface of a still pond—effortlessly, and without hesitation. I watch people jump from the windows of the upper floors, plummeting to their deaths on the sidewalk below. My mother's nutty emergency packing lists always include a flashlight, antiseptic, canned goods, and potable water, but never once has she reminded me not to forget my *parachute*.

It really messes with my head to know that nineteen guys thought it was a great idea to hijack passenger planes and blow themselves up along with thousands of innocent people. I stare at their pictures in the newspaper to see if I can detect it—a sign, a glimmer, something that reveals all that hatred. But their eyes don't glow red like the evil baby dolls in *Demonic Toys*. They're just normal guys. The world is a pretty fucked-up place.

Back at school we talk about matrix equations and subjunctive verbs while I wonder what those guys looked like as they boarded the planes. Were they nervous? Were they certain? I hear my classmates drone on about the symbolism of the chestnut tree in *Jane Eyre*, and another jumper plummets to the sidewalk in my head. Were their final thoughts of family? Were they scared to hit the ground? I listen to Great Eighters talk about silver charm bracelets and to my mother fret about the gas bill and to the politicians making speeches about how we were wounded, and how we will win.

I know there is more to life than shopping and gossip. There are droughts of hope and warring prophets, quests for change and truth. But it's not like I'm gonna march out of here tomorrow and start saving the world. I haven't even taken my PSATs yet. I'm not a genius, or a rebel, or Helen of Troy. I'm just stuck here, hovering above a hundred different worlds, each more absurd and surreal than its neighbor. The world in which my sister is a monkey, the world in which I'm queen of the train gang, the world where laudable achievements look like formulaic footnotes, and the world that is threatening to declare war on itself in a matter of days.

Then there is my pretty little lunch table of perfect popularity. As I feel myself drifting down an endless pink-petalled path of cocktail parties and sweet sixteens, a wild little naked girl within claws rabidly at the walls. Wriggles and shrieks. But there are no walls, and there's nothing to grab onto. So I drift on. I want to. Out of all the things that don't make sense anymore, the Great Eight makes the most. We're flawless. I've wanted to belong for so long, and now that I finally do, I'm not going to ruin it by getting all intellectual and introspective. So I shop and I gossip. The weeks fly by and nothing changes.

Last year, the Great Eight chose me. Now I choose them back—effortlessly and without hesitation.

chapter nine

DIETS SUCK

It is very easy to stay on track with my diet at school, as most of the girls have concocted their own rigid regimens. Cashmere drinks three sips of water and puts down her fork between every bite. One of the Bs is constantly raving about her nutritionist and personal Pilates coach. Some of the other girls even have gourmet organic meals delivered to their house each week.

"I've been on this fat flush where all you drink for seven days is, like, lemon water with cayenne pepper and this other secret ingredient, and it, like, *totally* detoxes your system," Teagan divulges before leaving to go to the bathroom.

The Great Eight girls count to ten in their heads—standard procedure whenever someone leaves to ensure a safe distance before tearing her apart. I always wonder why it doesn't occur to any of them that the ten-second rule applies to everyone, and that all bathroom breaks imply an imminent attack.

Cashmere takes the first swing. "What's the secret ingredient, *butter*?"

Teagan has gained weight since last year, and all the other girls seem to derive huge satisfaction from this. Glee, even. After she wins an award at Morning Meeting, her new tummy is the first topic of conversation at lunch that afternoon. Carbs are for the weak. Coffee has become its own food group. Nobody *ever* dares discuss dieting difficulties, only success stories. You are skinny and pretty or you're a fat failure, and there's nothing in between.

"Wonder if her grandmother docks her inheritance for every extra pound she gains!" one of the Bs exclaims.

"I love her, but seriously, her arms are disgusting," another B whispers as we spot Teagan returning from way across the dining hall.

"Whatcha talkin' about?" Teagan wants to know.

"Oh, nothin' too heavy," Cashmere tells her with a wicked grin.

You can tell a lot about someone's family when it comes time for driving privileges. After Cashmere nicks the paint on the BMW, Dot takes it for herself and buys Cashmere an enormous super-safety-conscious SUV, which she threatens will notify her if and whenever it goes over the speed limit. One kid gets a brand new Bentley for his fifteenth birthday, crashes it five hours later in an illegal license-less test drive, and then gets a replacement Bentley the next week. This one is red.

Meanwhile, I am stuck learning to drive in the clunky white minivan monstrosity that Dad purchased ten years ago with the transportation of Giant Tap Dancing Teeth, Giant Joke-Telling Potato Latkes, and Giant Singing Aliens in mind. Over time, a crusty red rust has crept from the corner of the side door all along the perimeter of the car, making it look two-toned from a distance. But its most distinctive feature is the sonorous guttural moan it lets out every time you make a right turn, which leads Cashmere and the rest of the girls to dub it "the Wookiee."

For driver's ed, everyone sits in a lecture hall facing a guy so ancient and lacking in personality that he might as well be carved out of the wooden podium he stands behind. We watch video after video of crash-test dummies catapulting through plates of shattering glass, and kids in flared pants from the seventies making "bad decisions" who end up in wheelchairs. Or dead. There's lots of death. Death by hydroplane, death by drunk driver, death by head-on collision. Julian and some of his buddies sneak in vodka in soda bottles and take shots every time someone dies. Even though it's kind of sick, after three months of class I'm tempted to join in.

It's our grade's first no-parents party, and I spend all after-noon choosing an outfit that will be both sexy and sophisti-cated. Over the course of the evening one of the Bs loses her virginity in the sauna, someone crashes a golf cart into a river, and I decide this is a good time to try and get drunk. Maybe if you're drunk you don't mind people shouting in your face and spilling Cosmopolitans in your hair. I sample beer, vodka, whiskey, and it all tastes like nail polish remover. I have to force myself to swallow even tiny sips without gagging. Remembering the rowdy high school parties I'd seen in the movies, I wait with anticipation for the part where I get giggly and start dancing on tabletops, but after the first drink I'm relaxed, after the second I'm sleepy, and well past my fourth

I just feel sick. I make my way to the bathroom and clutch the toilet as the tile melts beneath me.

Once I'm steady on my feet again I walk outside to get some air, where I find Teagan and a bunch of guys splashing around in the pool. They're an awkward scrawny bunch compared to Roberto, but at least they don't think I look like a turkey. Teagan declares she'll take her top off if all the boys drop trou, which they do. Then she snatches up their boxers and dashes into the house, with the boys in hot pursuit. I am left alone in the pool with Charles, my co-president from last year. It's dark. I think he's talking about Jimi Hendrix but I'm not really listening because I'm wondering if he can see that I haven't shaved my legs through the shimmery water. I think I like him. He kisses me up against the side of the pool and it's sloppy and wet, lots of tongue. *Is it supposed to be so wet?* He reaches up to feel my breasts. *Can he tell my bikini top is padded?* His hands grope and twist back and forth and back and forth and he's squeezing a little too hard and he—

"For God's sake, it's a breast, not a doorknob!" I hear myself say. So much for sexy and sophisticated.

When I eat only veggies and water for three days, my stomach flattens. Marvelous thin emptiness. But on the fourth day, when I reward myself with a real family dinner—my mother's famous hot open-faced chicken sandwiches—the gravy soaks into the pillowy soft bread, and it's warm and delicious. I eat until I'm satisfied. Until I'm full. Until two servings are gone, and then I pick up stray trails of savory gravy with my fork.

Three hours of homework tonight and three tests by the

end of the week, plus finals are coming, then Holiday Ball. The gorgeous gown Mom bought for me on clearance in the Garment District is getting tighter by the day.

"Hey, you wanna jam with me and Dad after dinner?" Sam asks. "I just learned this sweet new Miles Davis tune."

"Can't." I tell him. "No time."

The family clears the table, and I clean all the dishes to expedite their exit so I can have the kitchen to myself. Finally, when everyone is gone, I peek into the fridge. My father's wedge of lemon meringue pie beckons—puffy white peaks of sweet creamy decadence. I cut myself a little tiny sliver of a slice. Then another. Then just one more, to even out the other side, until I realize that half of the wedge has disappeared.

Idiot.

My diet is ruined.

I promise myself that I'll start fresh tomorrow. This will be my final carbo-riffic sendoff into the strictest diet I've ever embarked upon. I eat a bowl of warm maple oatmeal, then I want something salty—pretzels. Then I make a peanut butter sandwich, then I need just one more spoonful of pie. Taste, taste, taste. There is nothing but the taste, and everything is simple and soft as the chewy food massages the back of my throat.

"Who ate all the brownie out of the Ben & Jerry's?" Mom shouts.

I pretend not to hear her and continue working on my Spanish verb conjugations. Eighteen pages to go. *If I lose eighteen pounds by spring break, I'll definitely be back on track.*

Some people are born to teach. And some people are born to baffle, batter, and abuse the minds of students so thoroughly that as you watch each endless second tick by, you can actually feel yourself *un*-learning things you already knew. This year, most of my teachers are so astoundingly incompetent that by second semester I start to wonder if they are not crappy teachers at all, but rather brilliant extraterrestrials sent to sabotage the future leaders of the planet by melting teenaged minds from the inside out.

If the test is going to be a random amalgam of *anything*, regardless of what we discuss in class, then why have class at all? Why follow a schedule and give out homework? Why not just reach into a garbage bag filled with the pages from a shredded textbook and toss a bunch of scraps up into the air and test kids on those? Give them fourteen seconds. Turn off all the lights! Fill the room with balloons and strippers and rabid tigers. You'll get a circus of excitement to complement the thrill of staring into the baffled students' eyes as you wait to judge them on their lack of ability to read your fucking mind. Classes suck.

To make matters worse, the school has also hired a new "discipline-oriented" Dean of Students, Dr. Putnam, to make sure we stay competitive with other, more elite private schools. He instates mandatory academic detention for late homework and Saturday detention for being late to class three times. His most unpopular change, however, has nothing to do with academics. Putnam has banned flip-flops, and everyone from the jocks to the fashionistas is seething.

"What am I supposed to wear with *capri* pants?" Cashmere whines incredulously when Putnam announces the new decree.

Frankly, I don't give a damn, but I bring it up in the next student government meeting anyway just to see what Putnam will say.

"So, I can understand the need for a certain amount of modesty in the dress code," I begin tactfully, "but could we review this whole flip-flop policy again? None of the student representatives has voted for it, and I'm just not clear on what you—"

"*You*," he says, pointing around the room at all of the representatives, "are subject to my veto. Whether or not there has been a vote, flip-flops are heretofore banned. I will not have footwear compromising the academic efficiency of this institution. "

Mac, who is my copresident this year, raises his hand calmly, diplomatically. "With all due respect, sir, this committee usually reviews dress code revisions at the end of each year, so perhaps we can revisit this issue—"

Putnam is squat and bald, and now he's scowling something fierce, which makes him look an awful lot like Elmer Fudd on the hunt for "that wascally wabbit."

"Regular shoes produce one sound on impact," he says, stomping on the ground to demonstrate. "With a flip-flop, there are two distinct sounds. Twice the noise means twice the distraction."

"But—" Mac objects.

"Flip-flop. They make a flip . . . *and* . . . a flop."

Ian, who has been leaning back in his chair and covering his mouth to muffle his laughter, now takes the floor. "Dr. Putnam, I'm really glad you brought this to our attention. In fact, based on these concerns, I'd like to suggest a new barefoot policy. I think it'll really maximize hallway noise reduction."

Putnam glares at Ian. "Meeting. Adjourned."

Driving lessons with my mother always end with one or both of us screaming and vowing never to do it again.

"Left! You're veering leffft!" She grips onto the handle above the passenger window like we're in a jungle buggie about to drive off a cliff and into a lion colony.

"Mom, I'm *fine.*"

"You're—BRAKE! That guy is merging, you need to brake!"

"But everyone's honking at me!"

"Well, some people have a death wish." She rolls down the window and gives the guy behind us the finger. "She's a brand-new driver, asshole!"

I am mortified.

Dad takes a different approach. He tells me that "if you understand the physics, the, uh, dynamics of the movement of the car, you can negotiate any road. Let's parallel park."

"But Dad, I've never even—"

"We'll do it together. The thing you have to remember about parking is that it's all in the angles. Back up, and rotate to the right."

"But, Dad, I—"

"Back, back, back—"

Crunch.

Shit.

We get out to inspect the pole that seems to have jumped out of nowhere. Dad squints and rubs his stomach in circle. "Hmm . . . " He ponders. "Let's not tell your mother."

"Deal." *Well, that wasn't hard.* "She's totally gonna notice, though."

"But by the time she does, she'll probably think someone else hit it from behind."

I point to the distinctive crescent-shaped dent. "Someone shaped like a pole?"

Even though I've spent every single Saturday since September in driver's ed, my expansive knowledge of antiquated hand turn signals does not keep me from being stranded on the side of the road when I get a flat tire, or when my battery dies and black smoke starts pouring out of the Wookiee's hood. And when I get into my first car accident, not only do I have no idea what to do upon impact—apparently, screaming, "Fuckfuckfuck," at the top of your lungs and then bursting into tears is not exactly the professional approach—but I am also unaware that in New York, immediately admitting fault is pretty much the dumbest, most expensive thing you can do short of whacking a cop in the face with your newly detached bumper. The Wookiee and I are in big trouble when my parents' insurance premiums shoot up, so it looks like I'll be taking the train for a long time.

Driving sucks.

My weekend waitressing in the café is starting to suck too. A tray of decorative blue butter cream roses in the refrigerator sings its siren song whenever I pass by. If I've dealt with a particularly huffy customer, I find myself sneaking one or two creamy roses between breaks, until soon I have swiped so many that I have to rearrange the spacing of the remaining buds in order to hide their missing comrades. Eventually I need to take roses off of lower trays to replenish the original.

By the end of the semester, I'm pretty sure every single frosting decoration that was ever eaten by anyone in the shop was touched at least once by me. When the café shuts down, I'm glad for the opportunity to get a job with less delicious wares.

Amelia is picking flecks of dead skin off of my arm while I attempt to bargain hunt on eBay for another pair of fancy Seven jeans—the washing machine completely destroyed my first pair within two months. She grooms her way up my arm and shoulder, all the way up to my neck; it tickles a little, so I tilt my head away from her. I come across an auction for limited edition Sevens in my size, but the sloppy stitching in the picture smacks so much of crappy bootleg knockoffs that I can't help but laugh out loud.

"OW!"

Just as I begin to laugh, Amelia chomps down right on my jugular. I jump to my feet, knocking her to the floor, where she bristles, shrieking with anger. Even though she doesn't have teeth, Amelia's gums are so strong that she can leave a heck of a bruise if she's angry enough.

"Did you hurt Amelia?" Mom says, swooping in and gathering the little capuchin onto her lap, where she shrieks with renewed vigor.

"She bit my freakin' throat!"

"She was just playing."

"With my jugular vein?!"

I show my mother the bite mark. She reaches out softly to touch my arm, a rare display of physical affection. It's the closest my mother ever comes to a hug.

"Hannah, Amelia must have thought your laugh sounded like a challenge. Do you know what that means?"

"That she's fucking *psychotic*?"

"It means that Amelia thinks you're an adult! Isn't that wonderful? You've moved up in troop hierarchy!"

How thrilling. I march over to the sink to wipe Amelia's drool from my neck. Then I stomp out of the kitchen and grab the car keys. I'm meeting Cashmere and the girls at the mall.

"Honey, you have to stay and challenge her or else she'll think she can take advantage of you!"

Challenging Amelia requires gently but firmly pinning her arms to her sides while she shrieks and claws with her feet and bites at your hands until she finally decides that she's too tired to keep attacking. I'm going to have enough trouble explaining the one stupid monkey hickey I already have and I'm in no hurry to accumulate more, so I open the door to leave.

"Hannah, get back in here."

"I'm late."

"*Now.*"

"I thought Amelia said I was an adult!"

"You haven't even finished the dishes from last night, you've been stomping around here rolling your eyes all week, you boss your brother around like he's—"

"Fine." I stomp back up the stairs and turn on the sink as Mom approaches with Amelia, who lunges towards me and yanks out a handful of hair.

"What the hell?" I shout, "I'm not challenging you, I'm just doing the stupid dishes!" I take my hand out of the sink and flick water right into Amelia's face.

My mother gasps. "What is *wrong* with you?"

"You told me to challenge her!"

"That wasn't a challenge, that was just plain antagonistic. You know what? That's it. I don't want you hanging out with those bratty princesses again. Give me the keys. You're not taking the car tonight. You're going to Sam's piano recital with us."

"Fine. I hate that piece of shit car anyway."

I scrub the last of the dishes in silence and storm out of the kitchen. Amelia chases me down the hall to my room, where I slam the door. Hard.

"We're leaving for the recital in forty-five minutes," my mom calls from the kitchen. "I want you ready."

"Why don't you just take the fucking monkey?"

The first diet failed, the second diet failed, the third diet failed, but this time I will be strong. I sit in math class and feel my stomach growl. Nothing for breakfast, apple for lunch. I feel slightly euphoric as the class tries to find the value for x while I calculate something much more important: one apple at eighty calories twice a day for seven days, plus two dinners a week with my parents, means I'll lose . . . carry the two . . . three pounds a week. Plus exercise and, who knows?

As my restricting becomes more rigid, I find myself taking second, third, and fourth glances at the forbidden cakes and chocolates that I used to enjoy casually. Some days I eat absolutely nothing like the other girls at the lunch table. Other days I hoard piles of cookies in my locker and sneak mouthfuls between classes. It's embarrassing to be so adept at following other people's rules in school and so completely incapable of following my own for even a few days. I'm just going to have to try harder.

My shopping trips with the Great Eight have become disastrous. The slim pencil cuts that drape so gracefully around the Bs warp and bulge in hideous places on me, and my breasts push out the fabric of every dress I try on, hiding the contours of my waist and resulting in a wide cylindrical shape. The girls are kind enough to dub me "H-Battery."

I go on a juice fast and make a scrapbook of pictures I've cut out of magazines for motivation, for strength. Victoria's Secret models. Anthropologie. Abercrombie. I study their abs, their calves, their collarbones. Everyone knows that if two identical candidates are up for the same job, one skinny and one fat, the skinny person always wins out. I have to try harder. I must.

Twenty pounds before spring break, two inches before the big sweet sixteen party, one hundred crunches, three hundred calories, geometry, history, PSATs, binge.

"Hannah, listen to me very closely, because I'm only going to say it one more time: hell will freeze over before I pay to send you to Cancún."

"But, Mom, *everybody* else is going and I almost have enough money, I just need like four hundred more dollars."

"I'm not gonna give you *four* dollars. Do you know what shows up at spring break in Cancún besides pretty American tourists? Rapists and thieves. And El Niño. And if those don't kill you, the food poisoning will. Do you want to be mangled beyond all recognition by a—"

Dad clears his throat. "I think what your mother means to say is that we don't really feel comfortable with the idea, Hannah."

"She means to say we're fucking *poor.*"

After another month of begging, I get my mother to agree to let me go as long as I can pay my own way—she's positive I won't be able to make the money in time and is grateful to put the conversation to rest.

I take on extra waitressing hours at the new restaurant where I've started working, and I pick up steady tips for two months before I hit the mother lode. The entire back of the restaurant is being rented out for a huge corporate function, and I request a double shift to make sure that I get to cash in on what will likely be the biggest tip of my life—business dinners mean lots of drinking, and lots of drinking means a dinner bill way up in the thousands. Eighteen percent of two grand and I'll be on a plane to Mexico!

I spend six straight hours on my feet jetting between the kitchen and the back room, balancing steaming hot entrées and massive trays of booze. With every Jack Daniel's refill I deliver and each wolf whistle I ignore, I know that I'm another step closer to lying on a warm beach in a bikini having someone serve *me* a strawberry daiquiri. I'll need to really concentrate on my cardio routine to be able to get away with a bikini by spring break, but that's weeks away, and there's still two hours to closing, and by my calculations these guys already owe the restaurant enough to get me a hotel upgrade. Someone pinches my ass, and I'm about to spin around and tell him off when I remember the bikini and the strawberry daiquiri. I smile sweetly and hustle back to the bar to fill another round.

At the end of the evening the room is in shambles, but I know that the next two hours of vacuuming and cleaning will be worth it as I open the black leather folder containing their credit card receipt. There's nothing written in on the tip line. *Sweet.* Cash is even better—it'll be off the books. I move the paper aside to claim my prize.

One shiny copper penny.

My manager runs into me as I'm sprinting down the street screaming at the "cheap bastards" who screwed me out of a spring break, and my lucrative weekend shifts disappear along with any lingering dreams of strawberry daiquiris.

I write papers. I take math tests. I watch TV.

"Me and Tea are going to go to the City to check out that new Louis Vuitton store in SoHo. Wanna come?" Cashmere asks me one day at lunch.

I stop myself from telling her that I'd rather listen to whales mating for twelve hours than hear the girls discuss elaborate pre-bag expectations, dramatic bag encounters, and tearful post-bag farewells, but instead I tell her the truth. "No, thanks, guys. I'm kinda low on cash right now."

Teagan turns to me and shakes her head in confusion. "Duh, Hannah . . . just, like, write a freaking check."

Ian and I are sitting in the Dell after school one day while I wait for musical rehearsals to start. This year it's *Joseph*, and my harem girl costume seems to be getting smaller by the day.

"I feel like I'm gonna make an ass out of myself," I tell him. "All that wiggling around. It's embarrassing."

"You've got nothing to be embarrassed about, though."

"Easy for you to say. You're not gonna be in Spandex in front of the whole damn school."

"And I think we're all grateful for that," he says, adjusting his baggy shirt.

I spot a picture of some scantily clad supermodel on a fashion magazine Luna's using for a collage about patriarchy and the media. "Look at that!" I point. "What is that, like an *eight*-pack?"

"Who says you have to compete with that?" Ian asks.

"Nobody has to say it outright. It's just true. It's different for guys."

"Naw, guys have stuff, too—gotta be macho and built and all that." He puts his bare feet up on the table and rests his hands behind his puff of dandelion curls. "But the people who really, like, propagate that stuff are the ones who aren't comfortable just being themselves. You know?"

"I guess."

"What you need is a change of scenery," he declares, nudging my foot gently with his. "Seriously. Mountain Semester was such a breath of fresh air for me. I got to just take a step back and figure shit out, figure out who I was away from Danforth, the guys, my family, all of it. Breathing room."

"That sounds really nice."

"It was. You should look into it, kid. You deserve it. Fuck eight-packs."

The only thing I hate more than waking up bloated after a binge is having to rummage through my closet of secondhand crap to find something that doesn't look awful on me. It must be seasonal and sexy and tight enough to show off my new cleavage, but loose enough to conceal my sausage arms. It's impossible. I start canceling weekend invitations on a regular basis, preferring to sit in the peaceful dark of my room wearing comfy pajamas and watching sitcoms. Television women are radiant—impossibly thin, lean, beautifulbeautifulbeautiful. Sometimes I spend more time studying the calves of Neutrogena spokeswomen than studying.

I eat and watch. It is soothing, but in kind of a sickeningly sweet way, so I try not to think about it too much. Inevitably, my mother barges in with her eyebrows raised and hands on her hips to ask if I'm "*doing* anything on the weekend?" I'm not. *Get out.* I know that it's not normal to spend more time with Ben and Jerry than with my real friends, but having my mother rub it in truly confirms the fact that I'm hopeless.

I don't like throwing up. It makes my eyes water and my throat sting and it's very messy. Chunky food is hell to purge, as is anything spicy. The first and last time I binge and purge on Indian food, a piece of chicken tikka masala gets stuck in my nostril, and it burns so fiercely I am pretty much resigned to the idea that they're going to have to amputate my nose. I never mean to, but sometimes I find myself finishing a whole pint of ice cream, and then I churn and wriggle to get the ice cream to come back up again. Sometimes it's still cool and it's kind of soothing coming up, sweet and viscous, and I spit it back into the container until the container fills all the way up, up, up to the top again with creamy saliva bubbles. I am empty. I am disgusting, but at least now I'm empty.

Today Ian is missing from a really important student government meeting, and I'm expecting him to waltz in any minute bearing a big tray of cookies when Mac whispers that he's been expelled.

"What?!"

"I heard Putnam caught him smoking pot in the woods behind Rosewood."

Dr. Putnam has implemented a new zero tolerance policy, and although Ian has been an upstanding member of the community, a class president, and an all-around great guy with no previous offenses, Putnam ruins his chances of getting into a good college. Doesn't even let him say good-bye. The campus is devastated. People write petitions. Even teachers are appalled. But none of it does any good: Putnam stands firm. The following day at Morning Meeting, he announces that Ian was "cancerous to our community," and explains that it is "imperative to the integrity of our academic environment that students alert administration about other 'bad apples' who will 'spoil the bushel.'"

Mac starts calling him McCarthy. I'm pretty satisfied with just plain Putz.

More and more, as the year comes to a close, I start to see things from a different perspective. I observe myself from outside of myself, from the viewpoint of an invisible camera that zooms in unforgivingly on specks of dandruff, greasy blackheads, awkward gestures, and the roll of flesh that hangs over my jeans when I sit. I have to hide the imperfections lest they be exploited, discussed. The invisible camera follows me through the hallway and compels me to check my hair at any mirror I pass, to re-gloss lips and cover up the specks of possible pimples before they can be spotted.

After months of studying Scarlet and the other girls, the invisible camera begins to hover dependably above the lunch table. The mechanics of conversation, which, being the daughter of two social recluses, have eluded me my entire life, begin to reveal themselves to me like the gears in a clock. *Ask a question. Nod. Dirty story. Laugh. Question.* It's amazingly predictable. I feel like I'm operating a puppet from inside myself—a popular puppet. Marvelous me. I've finally met Hannah the Magnificent, but she's not who I thought she'd be. In fact, sometimes after I slip into costume, I hardly recognize her.

So I tug and I twist, always checking in with my invisible camera to make sure nobody sees the strings. *Question. Laugh. Make sure you don't have mascara goop in the corner of your eye. Are they bored? Am I boring? Do they see the little red bumps on my arms? Do they think I'm disgusting? Shitshitshit. Dirty joke. Ask a question.*

Silence.

They hate you. They think you're boring. They think your little red arm bumps are disgusting and that thing you said in English was stupid and . . . laugh. Laugh . . . laugh?

Make fun of Margaret. Yes. Margaret is disgusting. Margaret. Is fugly.

Today at Morning Meeting there is a presentation for an upcoming semester away program called CitySemester, an immersive-learning spring term that uses New York City as its laboratory and classroom.

Breath of fresh air. I feel like it's got to be fate.

I apply and get accepted. I imagine that waiting with anticipation for my Big Apple adventure will make the fall semester of junior year the worst I've ever faced at Danforth. And yet again, I'm totally wrong.

chapter ten

LOVE SUCKS

The artsy black and white photos papering every wall
of the photo lab speak to me. "Don't worry, Hannah," they
reassure. "Even someone as art-tarded as you can press a
button . . ." I envision myself stopping to inspect a lone dew-
drop, snapping pictures of tangled shadows and dead butter-
flies, a single wilting rose, a rending vision of mortality betwixt
beauty. Mostly, I'll have an excuse to wander around in dark
eye shadow with a camera around my neck, looking super
deep and contemplative. Everyone knows artists are *très* sexy.

Mom lends me her Nikon camera from college, and my first
roll of film is absolutely fucking brilliant. I go up into Dad's
tree house with long-stemmed glasses and a bottle of grape
juice that looks like red wine, a box of cigarettes I found in
the Dell, some candles and matches, and a lacy pink bra. I
snap a few shots of the bra draped dramatically over the
glasses. I light and then blow out the candle, capturing a
whisper of smoke hovering above the grape juice. It is brutally
artistic. I snap "Bra and Candles," "Cigarette and Seven

Matches Arranged in Circle," and "Bra Next to Shadow of My Torso," in quick succession. I'm, like, a genius.

"Why don't you take some pictures of Amelia?" my mother wants to know when I head back inside.

"Because."

"She's a very good subject."

"Ma, I'm not taking pictures of Amelia. I'm doing an artistic photo shoot."

"Amelia's artistic! Look!" Mom pulls Amelia's foot up next to her ear and mushes it into her face. "Picasso!"

When I develop the film, I am a little annoyed that my teacher does not break into applause and call a famous gallery right away to make room for my bright new visionary talent. "What are you trying to say here?" she says, pointing to my favorite print. "What do you want the audience to come away with?"

"I don't know, I just thought it looked interesting."

"For your next few rolls, if you're going to arrange a still life, really think about what you have in mind first." She holds my negatives up to the light and squints, staring at the edge of the sheet excitedly. "Is this—is this a monkey?"

"What?" I peek at the film to discover two rogue Amelia shots that Mom must have snapped when I wasn't looking.

"Yeah . . . that's Amelia."

"See, this is what I'm talking about! There's a perspective, a tone, an attitude . . . the monkey is such a stark contrast to this kitchen setting. It makes me want to know more!"

I force a smile and I nod. "Thanks."

"Keep trying with the still lifes, of course. I'm sure you'll get the hang of them eventually. But these monkey shots . . . Hannah, they're just fantastic."

Must. Kill. Monkey.

Junior year classes are brutal, and I have to step up my game. I'm sleeping less than five hours a night and I don't even have time to straighten my hair anymore. It bothers me terribly this afternoon because Adam has switched into the photo class, and I can feel him staring at my hideous frizz in the darkness.

"Check it out," Adam says, pointing to a dark paper floating in the fixer bin. "It's a rayograph: Saran Wrap and guitar picks," he explains proudly.

"Awesome," I say. A complicated cloud of fractals begins to emerge from the center of the picture as the chemicals seep in. We watch it together. He is so close I start to worry that I should have had a piece of gum after lunch.

He reaches out and twirls a piece of my hair with his finger. "Hey, would you mind doing me a favor?"

"What?"

"Would you lend me your hair for a second? It's nice when it's all curly like this. I think it would make a really cool picture.

" . . . Sure."

I follow him into the drying room. He takes out a piece of photo paper and drapes a section of my hair onto it gently. "Okay, don't move. I'm just gonna flick on the light for a second, and everything that isn't covered by the curls will get exposed."

We go back into the dark room and submerge the paper in developer. Slowly, broad white curls and playful squiggles appear against a lustrous black background like tendrils of fire.

Adam nods with satisfaction. "Pretty good, if I do say so myself."

"I wish they looked that good in real life," I joke.

He looks at me with a puzzled expression. "Women are crazy."

"What's that supposed to mean?"

"Just what it sounds like. My sister spends eighty bucks a bottle on hair shine cream and I can never tell the difference."

"You're saying I shouldn't use hair shine cream?" I pose playfully, walking past him to retrieve my negatives.

"No."

I turn. Without my glasses he only appears as a dark smudge on the other side of the room, but in the photo-safe red light I can see his teeth glowing. He's smiling. The smile approaches. "I'm saying . . . " step, step, "that all that shining and straightening is a waste of time."

I am bold. I reach forward and tousle his shaggy hair. "And what would you know about hair maintenance?"

He catches my wrist with his hand. "I know you look damn sexy in curls."

I feel my blood flutter, and my capacity for conversation flits out the door just as we're looking into each other's eyes and—

Blaring light pours in from the door. I skitter to busy myself at the photo developing machine behind me. Adam groans. "Goddammit, Trevor."

"Good to see you too, jerkoff."

"Close the door! The light overexposes all the pictures."

"Oh, my bad. Sorry, man, I didn't know you were working. I thought you were just, like, making out or something."

I carry around sheets of negatives in my homework folder and try for two weeks to orchestrate another alone-moment in the darkroom, but everyone is scrambling to get work done with midterms coming up. Cashmere is especially vigilant about keeping me company.

One day, Adam asks, "Wanna grab a cup of coffee after this?" *Finally.*

Cashmere intercepts. "Hannah and I are editing each other's English papers."

"Oh, you are, are you?"

"We are. And I suggest you stop dripping stop bath all over the floor. It's wasteful and it's a hazard."

"Thanks for the tip, blondie."

"Ugh." Cashmere slams her binder shut and marches toward the door. "Are you coming?" she asks me.

"Oh—yeah, just give me a minute."

"Well, I don't have all day."

"I'll meet you in the library, okay?"

"Fine."

Now things are quiet, save for the swishing of paper. Should I ask him to look at my pictures? Should I ask him about his day? After all of my planning and daydreaming, when we finally come face to face in front of the photo fixing basin the best thing I can think of to say is simply, "Hi."

"Hi," he says.

It's a breathless, gambling sort of moment, like when you're wondering if you have time to slip between the huge metal slabs of a closing elevator door before they crush . . . and we're kissing. It is fireworks and fairy tales, and then I remember that I have no idea what I'm doing. *Shit.* I realize I'm mannequin-stiff and decide to start moving my hands up and down his back, but this feels a whole lot like window washing. It is not sexy. I sort furiously through mental scraps of old *Cosmo* articles and *Sex and the City* episodes and try to remember techniques and tips they mentioned. Tongue swirling? Hmm . . . Cheek caressing? Lip nibbles?

"Ow," he says. "What was that?"

"Sorry! I don't know. I just—was it weird? Is this weird? Sorry."

"Don't be sorry. I kinda liked it. Just surprising, is all."

I raise my eyebrows provocatively. "I'm a surprising kind of girl."

He kisses me again, although truth be told I don't even feel like me. I am some sort of sex goddess princess in a big, flowy dress with heaving cleavage, and the music in my head swells to a thrilling climax of romantic strings as my prince whirls me into a low dip and—

"Ah!"

My foot slips in the stop bath puddle Cashmere warned us about, and when I try to catch myself on the counter, my arm lands in a vat of developer instead. It splashes everywhere.

"Are you okay?"

Other than being the most hopelessly ungraceful person on the planet, I actually feel marvelous.

He reaches to help me up, wraps his arm around my waist, brushes my hair behind my ear, and kisses me on the cheek. "I really like you," he whispers.

!!!

Adam stops smiling. "Is something wrong?"

"No! I mean, I like you, too! And I think I just—I need to

just rinse my arm off, it's kind of burning."

Later on in the library, Cashmere kindly informs me that I smell like old batteries. But even this, the bleach specks on my jeans, and having to wear long sleeve shirts for the next week to hide the scaly chemical burn on my arm do not diminish my absolute sheer fucking glee. Adam and I steal kisses in the darkroom after photo class and after lunch and after musical rehearsals. I even get a permanent spot in the Dell next to him on the couch, and we sit in a semicircle playing guitar, eating raw mangoes, and watching jittery little freshmen zip by.

The girls are furious that I've been ditching Great Eight events for photo lab make-out sessions. They make a point of insulting my newly relaxed fashion sense—curly hair, sandals, flowing skirts—at every opportunity.

> **ByootifulB:** hows it goin with Adam?
> **WritingHannah:** fine
> **ByootifulB:** hes not coming to my cocktail party next thurs though right?
> **WritingHannah:** um, ya I guess not
> **ByootifulB:** cuz its kind of, like, a formal affair, and I think one dirty hippie is more than enough
> **ByootifulB:** jk . . .

Julian is not thrilled with Adam, either, and refuses to even call him by his name.

> **JuliANT1social:** hows it goin w/ Adumb?

WritingHannah: shut up Julian

JuliANT1social: so does Adumb have that long hair
2 cver the lobotomy scar?

WritingHannah: you haven't even given him a chance!

JuliANT1social: pfd bhrrrrm

WritingHannah: that's not even a sentence

JuliANT1social: ur not even a stnecne

WritingHannah: are you drunk on a saturday morning?

JuliANT1social: bhrrrmm

Even Mac seems less than thrilled by my new romance.

Machiavelli1513: Ready to review, Friedman?

WritingHannah: aargh, sorry, i think i lost the sheet again.

Machiavelli1513: Perhaps you smoked it with your boyfriend?

Actually, I have yet to get high with Adam and his friends, but there's a first time for everything. And sometimes a second and a third.

I move into the dormitory toward the end of the fall semester because the commute is becoming overwhelming, what with musical rehearsals, after-school math tutoring, and my student leadership responsibilities. One night in the dormitory, I am thrilled to be addressed by queen hippie herself, Luna McClane.

"Yo, we're going down to the river," she whispers conspiratorially, her sari swishing around her ankles. "Adam wants you to come!"

This is a bad idea. Sneaking out of the dorms is punishable by expulsion. "I can't."

"Come on! We do it all the time."

"But what about the camer—"

"C'mere." She leads me into the hallway, walks right up to the security door, and quietly pushes it open. No alarm. She hikes up her sari and props the door with one foot while reaching up to the menacing grey camera mounted on the wall above the staircase. She flicks the side and a compartment pops open revealing . . . nothing.

"See? No tape," she smiles. "Just for show." She takes my hand. Before I have time to decide that this is really, truly an awful idea, I have already followed her out the electronically locked door, which will not open up again until 6 AM. If I swipe my student ID card for reentry, it'll register my name, condemning me automatically. I can't go back.

Now that I'm past the point of no return, breaking a huge, expulsion-worthy rule for the first time in my life, I realize why the cliché about hearing your own heartbeat exists. No matter how lightly I tiptoe, the thumping bass drum of my cardiac percussion has me sure that everyone in a two-mile radius hears us coming. But as we scurry down the hill and past the tennis courts, a giddy radiance comes pouring out from within, and I am shaking in a fit of hysterical giggles by the time we leap across the deserted main road and land in the lettuce patch of the house across the street, now completely and officially "off-campus."

I let out a small high-pitched shriek as I feel my phone vibrate.

"Chill out, babe," Luna laughs, touching my shoulder. "We do this all the time."

It's a text from Adam:

I'LL ROMANCE YOU BY THE RIVER WHILE WE MINGLE IN THE
MOONLIGHT, SO COME QUICKLY, KISS ME, MAKE MY NIGHT.

I can now die happy, content that I have lived my own fantastically romantic *Romeo and Juliet* story, even though our parents aren't warring and instead of killing ourselves at the end we're going to go make out down by the river. I'm startled when my phone vibrates again. Another text:

AND TELL LUNA TO BRING A LIGHT.

"He says to bring light?" I ask her.

She whips out a checkered lighter. "Lighter," she corrects. "You smoke weed, right?"

Shit.

D.A.R.E. training from middle school has resulted in a lot of drug-related confusion for me. I don't remember learning any real facts about the evils of marijuana, only watching a particularly vivid cartoon that depicted giraffe-sized joints and heroin needles with sharp teeth and bloodshot eyes chasing little kids around a darkened playground. As far as I could tell in sixth grade, a joint was just a taller, more tubular version of a demonic toy. Coincidentally, it is on a darkened playground where I first consider smoking pot.

A bunch of Adam's hippie friends gather around the bottom of a sunny yellow tube slide, taking turns ducking inside to shield themselves from the wind as they hold a lighter up to a glass pipe. I watch intently.

"You want to try some, babe?" Adam whispers as we watch Luna and her girlfriend, and Trevor and his flavor of the month, all playing on the monkey bars.

"Nah."

Too public, too sketchy . . . plus, what if we got caught? I pay close attention to the hippies. It's hardly reefer madness. They just giggle a lot and sometimes forget what they were talking about. They seem contented and connected to each other. I'm intrigued.

I Google pot. I find Erowid.org, an encyclopedic resource of drug knowledge, and I read all about the chemistry of tetrahydrocannabinol, the main psychoactive ingredient in weed. I'm surprised to learn that there has never been a documented cannabis overdose, that it's far less addictive than alcohol and caffeine, and that it's been used medicinally for over four thousand years. The forums say that cannabis is a miracle crop that can be grown without pesticides and used for food, fiber, and fuel. Apparently, it was publicly demonized in the 1930s because textile bigwigs began to feel threatened by its enormous potential. Some claim the outlawing of cannabis was also a blatantly racist response to its popularity with Mexicans and blacks. I research its history and find that George Washington and Thomas Jefferson grew cannabis on their personal farms, that it was such a useful commodity in colonial times you could use it to pay your taxes, and that the Declaration of Independence was even drafted on hemp paper.

I read dozens of personal accounts about getting high. Some describe giggly flights of fancy, while others detail very scary fits of paranoia. But nobody goes crazy forever or starts craving massive amounts of heroin. Hmm. . . .

"So, tell me what it's like again," I prompt Adam as he takes out a clear plastic bag filled with a clump of greenery and lays it on my bed.

"I don't know, babe. It's just, like, a different perspective."

"And it's not dangerous?"

"No more dangerous than alcohol." He considers. "Probably less so, actually."

"But what about the stuff I read about people really freaking out?"

"I don't know, honey. It's not for everybody. I've never seen that happen, but I don't think you should try it if you have doubts."

I do have doubts. I'm a good girl with good grades who won the D.A.R.E. essay competition in sixth grade. I unzip the baggie and study the dried green clump of leaves. It looks pretty harmless, I guess. I think about the giant, evil giraffe-joint chasing little kids around the dark playground and feel confused. Nobody ever told me about the history of cannabis, the science, the political machinations . . . just that it was bad, bad, bad, period.

I really like Adam. I trust him. We've been going out for three months now. I've seen his friends get high, and it looks like fun. They're not delinquents or drug addicts. They just sit around talking and laughing, eating Cheetos. I think I want to try pot. I've done the research and I'm pretty sure it will be okay to try it just this once. I'm nervous, but I want to try it.

Adam crumbles some of the bud onto the cover of my calculus textbook, then distributes it evenly into the crease of a thin white rectangle of rolling paper.

He folds one side around the pot, rolls the cylinder back and forth between his thumb and forefinger, and then deftly wraps it all the way back toward the other end of the paper.

"This end is sticky," he explains, licking the edge and sealing the joint.

He passes it to me and I inspect it carefully. No sharp cartoon teeth. I see him take out the lighter. Suddenly, I get a flash of my parents bursting in while I convulse on the floor, foaming at the mouth and speaking in tongues. Drugs are bad, bad, bad. *Stop freaking out.*

"Want me to show you?" Adam asks.

I nod.

He puts the joint in his mouth and flicks the lighter, bringing it toward his face. Lights. He inhales. The smoke smells sweet. He passes it to me. *Now or never.* I bring the joint to my lips and inhale. The smoke is irritating. I cough and cough. I can't stop coughing.

"Don't worry," he smiles reassuringly, patting my back. "That happens to everybody."

Cough, cough. "When will I feel something?"

"You might not on your first time."

And I don't. I don't feel anything on the first time or the second time. The third time, I'm hanging out with Adam's hippie friends. I like them. They don't talk about college applications or purses, and they all seem very relaxed in their own skin. Trevor is having a party, but there's no screaming and puking like at Teagan's parties, or blinis and beluga caviar like at Cashmere's. Just chill music and a bonfire. A bong as tall as me reflects warm colored light in the corner of Trevor's room.

"That's Bong Marley," Adam explains.

"Naw, man," says Luna, "that's Long Bong Silver."

Trevor corrects them. "You're both wrong." He strokes the smooth reddish glass affectionately. "Her name is Pippy Bong-stockings, and I expect you to treat her with some respect, dammit." He smiles.

We light a campfire in the backyard and toast marshmallows and eat Doritos. They all pass around a glass pipe with a little tuft of pot in the end of it.

It's good to see Ian again. I've missed our Dell chats and his dependably sunny sense of humor, which always managed to make Great Eight drama seem not so important. I've heard he's been having a hard time adjusting to a new school. I watch him. He smokes with abandon.

"Marshmallows!" Trevor's dad wanders outside with another bag of marshmallows, and conversation shifts to roasting technique as we pass around the candy fluff.

Ian takes a hit off of the bowl and passes it to me.

I flick the lighter over and over, but it keeps getting blown out in the wind. Adam shields the bud with his hands and I inhale deeply. Once, twice, thrice, and I turn to pass the bowl to Adam.

"No, babe, you keep it for a little while."

"Hey, hey, hey, what the hell are you talking about? Pass that shit!" Trevor shouts through a marshmallow-stuffed mouth.

"Take it easy, Trev. She's a newb."

Everybody stops talking.

"You've never smoked pot before?" Luna asks excitedly. "But I thought—"

"Well, I tried it a few times, but nothing happened."

"So you've never been high?!"

140

"Lay off, Luna," Adam says defensively.

Luna prances behind my chair and drapes her arms around my neck. "No, no, I'm not teasing. I just think it's cute! This is so exciting! I can't wait for you to—"

"Eh, what the hell happened to puff, puff, pass people?" Trevor asks. "I don't care if this is your first time on Planet Earth, sweetheart. The whole damn universe knows it's puff, puff, pass."

"Don't listen to him, honey. Take your time," Luna coos, stroking my hair.

Adam takes my hand and kisses it. He winks at me. I smile.

I inhale. In . . . out . . . in . . . out. Again . . . I—oooh.

Slowly, my smile is undeniable, and my chair is a marshmallow. The fire is dancing, is crackling, is man's red flower . . . A warm, fuzzy light softens the usual nibbling, nagging, pinching nerves in my head. I listen to Luna laugh. Ian laughs. I laugh. We all laugh and smoke and watch the fire flinging wisps of dazzle into the air. Through the shimmering heat above it, everyone looks warm and distorted. I feel . . . comfy.

The invisible camera that has followed me so critically for so many long months suddenly swivels away from my frizzy hair. It frames colors and gestures and fleeting moments of beauty. Luna's lovely, lovely laugh. Ian's cacophony of curls. I fit my fingers into Adam's hand and live inside the warmth and want to write songs. I notice the intricate brickwork on the patio . . . mosaics. Macedonia. My camera captures all.

Ian sighs. "I miss you guys."

I want to hug Ian, help Ian, thank him for listening all those times.

"I can't believe they kicked you out without so much as a

warning," Adam tells him, passing the bowl. "I mean, it could have been any one of us. Remember freshman year in the dorm when we used to hotbox our closet? I figured they always knew and didn't really care."

Ian takes a hit and laughs. Thinks. Shakes his head. "It sucks, dude. My parents don't even trust me to go to the grocery store on my own. Now it's like, unless I go into medicine or the priesthood, my brother will be the lawyer and I'll be the eternally irresponsible disappointment."

I want to say everything. I pass Ian a marshmallow because he's sad and he's my brother.

"At least you're not a *gay*, irresponsible disappointment," Luna quips. "My dad hasn't looked me in the eye since I came out."

"Speaking of gay," Trevor interrupts, "did you see that spectacular lesbian action in the lounge this afternoon? That shit was hot."

Luna rolls her eyes. "I hate fair-weather gays. They decide they're bisexual to get back at Daddy, and then the minute they feel a drop of persecution, they go running home to their Easy-Bake Ovens and white weddings. Scarlet pulled that shit all the time last year."

"I seem to remember her pulling that shit all the time with *you*, on the baseball field, after lights-out, if memory serves . . . " Trevor smiles naughtily.

"Well, that was before she went off the deep end," Luna explains.

"Crazy or not, that shit was hot."

Luna chucks a marshmallow at Trevor, and he catches it in his mouth.

Adam shakes his head. "I don't know, I always felt a little bad for her. I think she was lonely. One of those 'look at me' types, ya know?"

"Yeah," Luna sighs, remembering. "She was super worried about what everybody thought . . . I think it became all-consuming."

"She shoulda been consuming my cock," Trevor snorts.

Luna smacks Trevor in the arm.

"Or at least a freakin' sandwich."

I laugh so hard into the bowl that I blow a little comet of flaming bud right out of it, and it lands on the ground. I expect to feel embarrassed, like the time I ruined the caviar at Cashmere's house. But my shoulders feel loose and low, my future is bright bright bright, and my invisible camera is far too busy enjoying the chorus of fireside crackles and the glow of a hundred billion stars overhead to notice insignificant things like proper etiquette. I just don't care. Apparently, neither does anyone else.

"Don't worry, babe," Adam says, patting my leg. "That was just our starter bowl."

chapter eleven

SEX SUCKS

Math sucks, AP test prep sucks, stupid Danforth Academy politics suck, but kissing is *fantastic*. Adam and I start dating officially, and I have to keep pinching myself to believe I have a boyfriend. A talented, funny, handsome, older boyfriend whose lips are soft and who has a car and plays guitar. After a while I stop picking out special outfits for Adam. I wear my comfy sweats and we snuggle and watch movies and talk about our dreams. We want to be different from our parents in so many ways, but exactly like them in all the good ones. We want to run away to Mexico and tear up all our homework. He writes me poetry and we kiss in the photography darkroom and I tell him my secrets. When we snuggle, I fit into the nook of his chest perfectly. When we're together in his car, speeding down the highway blasting Dylan and Marley, I put my bare feet up on the dashboard and wear my gas station sunglasses as the stresses of school fade into the background, and everything is just groovy. It still feels like I'm biding my time, like I'm just jumping through hoops waiting for the real world to start, but now that Adam and I are together, I don't feel like I'm trekking through the labyrinth alone anymore.

It's not always just the two of us, though. More and more when we're making out, we are graced with guest appearances from a big erection, which sticks up from his colorful boxers like a circus tent. It's super awkward, and I wish it would just go away. I like Adam and he makes me feel safe and comfortable, but this . . . this thing is not part of my equation. When I was younger, I sometimes thought about losing my virginity to a blue-eyed prince with rippling muscles who gallops over on a white steed, but my fantasies always ended with a big finale kiss and never quite progressed into the messy logistics of weird erections. Now I just wish his penis would disappear, because it keeps popping up uninvited in the middle of perfectly lovely, innocent, half-clothed kissing sessions.

Adam is very intent on pleasuring me in bed, but the more he tries, the less I'm pleased. Over-pajama rubbing was tingly and fun, but when I let him go under my pants, he pushes with sharp fingernails and rubs my clitoris like a scratch-off lottery ticket.

"Ow! Not good!"

"Ooh, sorry, babe. How about this?"

" . . . that's just *weird*."

"Well, show me what to do then."

My parents are surprisingly cool about Adam coming over. I think my mother figures I'll get into less trouble in the house than out of it. This proves to be a very wise philosophy because everything about sex is confusing and exciting and scary and awkward enough without having to worry about secret forest trysts that result in picking ticks off your boyfriend's balls, or BMW make-out sessions that end abruptly when someone's ass accidentally knocks the stick shift out of park. Teagan says she's jealous of my parents' low-key attitude and advises me never to give a blow job in a moving car.

I Google blow jobs. I make categorical notes like in history class, except that now the Political, Economic and Social headings are replaced by Pressure, Enthusiasm, and Spit. No teeth. Variation. Ball rubbing? *Eiw.* The next time Adam comes over, I feel more like a deep sea diver than a sexpot as I take his wrinkly pink salamander neck in my mouth and start to move it in and out like it says on the websites. He moans and I feel a pulsing, and it stiffens even more.

"Faster," he whispers.

I oblige. Weird. I have a penis . . . in my *mouth.* What would my grandmother say? *Eiw, eiw, eiw, don't think about Bubby. That's just disgusting.* Think about something sexy. Like . . . *wait, is it supposed to smell like this?* I notice the pile of laundry in the corner of my room. *I have to ask Mom about that detergent . . . the unscented kind . . . I think the lint trap is still broken.*

"Oh, God, that's so good," he moans.

I slow down and speed up and lick all the way along the shaft and then concentrate on the head. I feel like my mouth is running a fucking marathon. In, out, in, out. I watch five whole minutes pass on the digital clock. Six. My jaw is aching. Seven. Ten.

"Baby, that's amazing."

Then what the hell is taking so long? I resolve to quit just as several spasms of spunk spurt into my mouth. Ugh. Semen tastes like saltwater pudding. I try to hide my sour face, but I quickly realize that my jaw is cramped open. Fuck. It comes out sounding more like "huck."

"Are you okay?"

"Huck."

"What?"

"Is*shtuck.*"

I scream. I start bouncing up and down on the bed, shaking my arms, and then my mother shouts from the kitchen, "Is everything okay?"

"Yesh!"

"Is everything okay?" She's outside the door now. "I heard a scream."

"I'n hine."

"Are you sure?"

"I'n *hine!*"

"Well, you don't sound—"

"I'n okay, I'n okay." I want to say, "*Good-bye,* Mom," but realize that I won't be able to pronounce the "b" or the "m," so I just hope she takes the hint and leaves. She does. After a minute or so, my mouth muscles relax. I curse the online chat forums in my head.

The next day I make the mistake of telling one of the gay guys in the musical with me, who thinks it is absolutely hilarious, and of course by the end of the day half of the grade is giggling as I walk by.

Teagan is nice enough to come up to me after rehearsal. "Heard you had, like, a tricky time last weekend. The secret is," she makes a circle shape with her thumb and forefinger, "you gotta use your *hand*. Very important. Good grip will get them off like *that*," she says, snapping her fingers. "Actually, both hands is really the way to go. Get some, like, ball-cupping action going, let your middle finger roam a little . . . and then the tongue is just for, like, embellishments and stuff." I am mortified. It's the Kotex in the gas station all over again, except now it's the entire school watching, and the item in question is a penis. Perfection.

Adam eats like an Olympic swimmer, and it's impossible for me to stick to my diets when he's around. How do I expect to be successful in life if I can't do something as simple as stop eating so damn much? It's humiliating. I'll do better. I pore over formulas like an alchemist: low protein, no carbs, high cardio . . . it all seems so easy, yet nothing works. After an entire year of crazy crash diets, I weigh way more than when I started, and I am beginning to feel like the biggest failure with the least self control of any miserable fatty on the planet.

Twenty-five pounds before bikini season, eight hundred crunches, sixty calories, SAT prep, binge.

Eating habits and oral sex aside, Adam and I are fantastic together. We get high in the forest and write poetry, and he does charcoal drawings of my breasts and plays guitar to accompany my homework-doing.

"Babe?"

"Babe, I'm doing homework," I tell him, shuffling between thesis drafts.

"Let's run away together. Thailand."

"Don't be ridiculous."

"I'm not being ridiculous. Let's really do it this time."

"You're crazy."

He sneaks up behind me and kisses me on the neck. "Crazy for you."

I make a sarcastic "Are you kidding me?" face, but secretly I think he is amazing, amazing, amazing.

"Have I ever told you how beautiful you look all studious like this?"

I'm going to marry him. Hannah Cole. Hannah Friedman-Cole. Hannah I-don't-even-care-that-half-the-school-has-heard-about-my-blowjob-disaster-because-I-think-I-might-be-in-love Cole.

Adam prides himself on being the black sheep of his family, which includes seven kids and two loving Mormon parents. Although he's always thrilled to partake in fancy family vacations, he openly abhors country club lunches and goes to great lengths to wear sandals and grumble about capitalistic decay as often as possible. His parents are really, really nice. Like, pod-people nice. One time his mother even insists that I borrow one of her dresses for a cocktail party we're going to. Adam's dad is an ex-stockbroker who got out while the market was still good. He's one of those guys who runs marathons and builds sailboats and credits his success to the Lord and a high-protein diet. Adam admires him but doesn't want to be like him. "Bob's all work, ya know? He just goes and goes and goes and doesn't ever stop to look around. Everything's so *literal* with him."

Adam invites me to his family's annual Christmas dinner. He's going to pick me up from my aunt's house, where we're having our nondenominational holiday Chinese food meal. We're watching old episodes of *South Park* and my mother is regaling the family with a thrilling tale of monkey diarrhea while we eat gloopy Chinese food, which suddenly seems much less appetizing. Sam reaches over me to serve himself and ends up spooning more General Tso's sauce onto my dress than onto his plate. "Dude!" I tell him. "I gotta look decent tonight." I am wearing my velvet dress, which makes me stand out among my pajama-clad family. I spit on the General Tso's stain and try to rub it out with a napkin.

Adam picks me up, looking as handsome as ever. I never thought I'd like him better in a tie than in his usual casual hippie getup, but something about this outfit is distinguished, manly . . . hot. We drive to his house and make out in the car until his cell phone rings, startling us.

"Ah, it's my mom. She wants to know where we are. You ready?" he asks, offering me his hand as I get out of the car.

"Wait, so one more time," I review. "Don't let Aunt Betsy talk me into giving her a drink, stay away from the twins, and I shouldn't be surprised if Nana Cole thinks I am personally responsible for the death of her Lord and Savior."

He kisses me on the nose. "Yeah, she's kinda crazy. You're amazing. Let's do it."

Both of Adam's parents have eight or nine siblings apiece, and although Adam had warned me about his seventy-two first cousins, it didn't sound like quite so large a number until all of their little blonde heads snap simultaneously to look in my direction as we walk in the door. I'm at *Children of the Corn* Christmas. In the Cole mansion, I stick out like a gooey slab of gefilte fish on a platter of angel-shaped Christmas cookies.

Nana Cole is kind enough to tell me so. "Merry—you've got a spot on your dress, dear. Merry . . . wintertime," she rasps.

The men sit in the dining room drinking scotch and talking stocks and sports and politics, while the women dart back and forth between the dining room and the kitchen making playful jibes at their husbands, serving cocktails, and arranging platters of pepper crackers and baked brie.

Awkward introductions aside, the thing I'm most surprised about—and then feel ashamed for being surprised about—is how normal everyone is. They're really warm and lovely and friendly. They sing songs and tell stories and take pictures of all the dozens of cousins by the fireside. They drink eggnog and wear cute little red bows. It's adorable. Now it's more like I'm in a heartwarming *Leave It to Beaver* Christmas special, except that Adam keeps trying to feel me up in the pantry.

"Stop that!" I giggle. "Be good. I feel like your grandmothers are watching my every move."

"Well, they haven't tried to sacrifice you to a golden Santa statue yet, so I think you're probably in the clear . . . Although my aunt did ask to see your horns."

"You think you're hilarious, don't you?" I tickle him under the arms until he bursts out laughing. Someone starts playing "White Christmas" on the piano outside and he catches both of my wrists, guiding my hands around his neck and pulling me into his chest. We sway a little.

"This is fun," I whisper.

"You sound surprised."

"Oh, c'mon, the way you described Cole Christmas it sounded like a nativity nightmare."

"Well, I don't remember the last time it was this much fun. And everybody loves you."

"Stop it."

"No, really!"

"How do you know?

"Because," he lifts my chin up and kisses me so lightly on the forehead, " . . . I love you."

Adam's mother bursts in carrying a tray of hors d'oeuvres. "Oops!"

Fuck. "Hi, Mrs. Cole! We were just—"

"Ah, look at you two, aren't you just adorable! Reminds me of when Bob and I were first going steady, always sneaking off to be alone . . . And Hannah, you are just the talk of the evening! Everyone adores you."

Adam nudges me playfully.

"But you two better get out here, we're circling up."

Suddenly he looks concerned. "Umm . . . Mom, don't you think Hannah and I should—"

"Nonsense."

"But she—"

"I'll see you *both* in the circle." She grabs a can of artichoke hearts and winks at us before leaving.

Adam bites his lower lip and then spins me to the other side of the pantry. "We really gotta start locking doors."

"What did you say?"

"I said we really gotta start locking—"

"Before that."

He grins.

"Say it again."

"Hannah Friedman, my sweetest, most passionate profundity, princess of the pantry . . ."

I jab him in the side.

He looks at me. "I love you." We kiss.

"I love you, too." And the lights soften and the music swells and we're locked in a magnificent fairy-tale kiss, a Disney kiss, a golden-ball-gown-magical-rose kiss, and it's the most fantastic thirty seconds of my life. All too soon, however, we hear people looking for us outside, and we sneak out to join the rest of the family in the living room.

A hundred chairs have been arranged in a large oval next to the most beautiful Christmas tree I've ever seen. This is the real deal—tasteful twinkling fairy lights illuminating fragile antique ornaments and delicate teardrops of painted glass, topped by a lace-winged angel and surrounded by hill after shiny hill of perfectly wrapped presents. This tree looks like it should be in a museum or the White House or something.

Adam and I take a pair of empty seats just as his father, clad in a cheery reindeer sweater, stands to announce, "Family! I feel eternally blessed to be spending another joyous holiday in your warm company. We gather once again by the grace of God to celebrate and to reflect on the blessings and joy he has brought unto us. Amen."

"Amen," everyone says. Adam takes my hand.

Okay, I can do this. It's like in Hebrew school—you just have to say amen after everything anybody says. And so I do. I say amen after a couple of speeches and then after some hymns and again after some more speeches and then after some carols and even after an original poem. Finally, just when I think we're about to be done, Adam's dad announces,

"And now, as is tradition, we will go around the circle and share what we each love about our personal Lord and Savior."

Uh-oh. I dig my nails into Adam's arm as one by one people share stories and songs about faith and joy. As my turn draws closer, I start to panic. I desperately fumble for pieces of New Testament stories I've seen on TV. Lions? Lepers? Wine? Umm . . . can I pass? I look at Adam to try and communicate my panic. Suddenly, it's my turn. A sea of blue eyes all fixed on me. *Fuck. Double fuck.*

Adam stands. "Ahem." He loosens his tie. "Hi there, family! It's wonderful to have you all here. Really, I can't express what a joy it is to share this evening with you. And I only wish we could get together like this more often without having to hide beneath the guise of a bastardized, consumerist vestige of a once-meaningful day that no longer has anything to do with the original ideals Jesus preached! You know why Santa's so fat?"

A cherubic little toddler exclaims, "Presents!"

"That's right, Jacob. He's been gorging himself on the greasy haunches of materialism and corporate greed while the Virgin Mary shivers away in a manger. *Weeping.*" He sits down. Mouths are agape. *Jesus Christ.*

Later, out on the front porch, I confront Adam. "What the hell was that? Your family was being so loving and sweet and then all of a sudden you start raging about *consumerism?*"

"Well, everybody else was being sweet. It was a much-needed change of pace."

"It was a disaster! You sounded like the most ungrateful, sour—"

"I know!" He grins. "And that whole greasy Santa part at the end, I mean, that was off the cuff, but it was just *inspired*."

"You think that was funny? It was terrible!"

"Oh, c'mon, they're used to it. I whine about consumerism every year. They knew I was kidding."

"Are you mental? They were horrified! Your aunt almost choked on a candied walnut!"

"Ooh, there are candied walnuts?"

"Are you even listening to me? I mean, after that little stunt I could've done a striptease with Star of David pasties and nobody would have even noticed!"

He kisses me on the nose. "Exactly."

Oh. "You unbelievable *bastard*." I smack his arm. "If you had told me you were going to do that I would have—"

"You'd have tried to talk me out of it. I didn't want to worry you."

"What is wrong with you? You're crazy!"

"You're beautiful."

"That was *crazy*."

I can see whispers of his frosty breath as he leans in and squeezes my hand and tells me, "Merry Chanukah, Hannah."

We stand there nose to nose, palm to palm, kiss after kiss, shivering on the empty porch in the fresh snow. I squeeze his hand back.

"Happy Christmas, Adam."

Just my luck, after a few fabulous months of being in love, Adam and I are torn apart by our respective semester away programs. He's headed for a mountaineering semester out west, and I'm packing up for CitySemester. I am beyond devastated. We are the perfect team, a dynamic, poetic duo of destiny. He lends me novels about magic and time-traveling soul mates and tantric sex. I read him my short stories and we spend long weekend afternoons in bed getting high and listening to music. We are absolutely the best snugglers in the history of the world.

Because our programs don't start until late January, we enjoy a luxuriously extended winter break, during which we sleep late and make omelets and watch movies and feed the ducks by the train station and tease each other about our crazy families and listen to good jazz. I feel like I'm in the happy part of a Woody Allen movie.

One week before Adam has to leave, all the constellations align. My parents are away for the evening. I haven't binged this week, so my stomach is flat. I'm ready. I think I'm ready. I take a shower and shave my legs and feel the soft weight of my breasts in my hands and wonder what it's going to be like. I dry off and try on three different outfits. I want to be sexy but casual. This one is too casual. And this one is too vampy. Too matchy. I mean, I'm going to remember this forever, so it has to be—I realize I've spent half an hour picking out clothes that I only intend to be wearing for the five minutes before I take them all off. This insight narrows down the choice significantly, and I settle on brown linen hip-huggers and a tight white top. Then I decide that white might be too weirdly symbolic and go with turquoise instead. I wait.

I make my bed neatly and arrange the mosquito netting draped from the ceiling around it. I light candles. I do sit-ups. I decide to write a song. This is the perfect time. I have tried to write songs many times before but have always gotten frustrated with myself and stopped halfway because the chords weren't right, or they sounded a little like something already written, or my lyrics were dumb and circular. But now I have the perfect reason to write. A poetic reason: it'll be my *virgin* song. And when they interview me about it on *E! True Hollywood Story*, I'll tell them about picking out my outfit and being nervous and they'll play the clip, which will be tender and innocent, but also wise and wonderfully poignant.

Or at least it would be if it consisted of more than one chord: E. I alternate between E and C . . . too corny. E and G? Boring. E and something really crazy? A tritone? I try to jazz it up with diminished chords and flat fives, but it sounds like I'm trying to be avant-garde. Maybe the music will come once I get the lyrics down. But the only thing that rhymes with virgin is . . . sturgeon. I hate this song. It sucksucksucks. I am nervous, and I feel like if I chronicle this moment artfully, it'll be a meaningful adult observation instead of the hysterical ramblings of a silly fluttery-stomached kid. But I never make it past the E. Songwriting sucks.

Adam shows up with some popcorn and a DVD, which I watch with him in the living room without really watching. For the first time in months, I am nervous. I smile too much. I look toward the wall and bite my lip and close my eyes and wonder.

"Hey," he says, brushing my hair behind my ear, "what's going on in there?"

"Nothing. I'm just tired."

"Wanna go to sleep?"

"No. I mean, well—" I kiss him fiercely and lead him into my bedroom, where we roll around and make out. His arms are familiar and safe, and I look into his eyes and tell him, "I want to."

"Are you sure?"

"I want to."

He springs out of bed like a cartoon character and goes over to his backpack in the corner. He returns with a condom and a floppy penis. He frowns. "Ah, I—"

I pull him back onto the bed, secretly glad that I'm not the only one in over my head. I kiss him and make my way down to his neck and lower. He breathes heavily. When it's ready again, I sit back against a pillow and stroke his ankle encouragingly as he tears at the condom wrapper. He extracts the ring of rubber and tries to unroll it one way, then another with his fingers.

"Aren't you supposed to—"

"I got it." He unrolls the condom all the way like a droopy sock and then tries frantically to stretch it as quickly as he can over his slowly deflating member. The latex is uncooperative. "Fuck."

"Don't worry," I say.

"I hate these things."

"What do you mean?"

"I mean they're always so impossible to—"

I pull the sheet up to my chin. "Wait, you said you were a—"

"Oh! No, no, you're my first. I wanted to do a dry run before we . . . " He looks down, stretching out the condom width-wise and trying to shove in a bundle of skin. "Though it doesn't look like the practice made much of a difference." Stretch. "Damn." He frowns at his floppy penis. He looks like a sad clown.

I try to suppress it, but I start to giggle a little. A lot.

"Oh, you think this is funny?"

"A little."

"Yeah, well, it's harder than it looks."

I can't help myself. " . . . Apparently not."

"Oh, that's it, you asked for it!" He puts down the condom and launches a tickle attack. I retaliate with a pillow thwack, and we giggle and roll around the bed and laugh and laugh and kiss, until suddenly the door bursts open like the Gestapo kicked it down.

I scream and jump under the covers, and Adam sits there frozen as I peek out my head to see who it is. But there's nobody in the doorway, only a little monkey frantically scrambling to pull herself up onto the bed.

Adam covers his crotch with a blanket. "Holy shit! How did she do that?"

Dammit. "She doesn't like the sound of my laughing. She thinks it's a threat."

"That was nuts!"

"Amelia, get out! Out!"

We chase her around the room, but she is unusually spry this evening, darting this way and that, shrieking and clawing and knocking over lamps and bottles and finally a candle. It starts to singe a small section of my mosquito netting until Adam leaps to douse it with a glass of water and I smother it with a blanket, bringing the whole meshy mess down onto our heads. Amelia hoots triumphantly and darts off the bed, leaving a pile of monkey poop behind her before skittering out the door.

Adam and I sit naked beneath the tangle of mosquito netting. "Wow," he says, untangling himself with his arms. "Well. I've never been cock-blocked by a monkey before."

The next time we try to have sex, things don't go any better, and this time I can't blame the monkey. Adam gets the condom on (I was right about not unrolling it all at once), but when he tries to go inside of me, I'm startled by the pain. He stops. "Baby, we don't have to."

"No, I'm okay, really," I tell him, figuring that after the initial sting things won't be so bad, kind of like getting a shot. I don't even know if what follows counts as sex because everything just burns like hell. I'm not sure if he's inside of me and he doesn't cum, just goes soft after a while. I say, "Don't worry about it, babe," but really I'm thinking, "Thank God."

It's two days before Adam leaves and this time we're going to get it right. Seriously. He glides his hands along my waist and envelops me in his strong arms like he is a warrior and I am his princess. His chest is warm, and he kisses me on the forehead softly, lingering.

"Luna said that I should . . ." He trails off, resting his hand between my legs, separating and probing, and after a while we try again. He still doesn't cum. The next time we try he goes for much longer and keeps asking me what feels good and what he should do, but all I can think about is how much I wish he would just cum quickly and get the hell off. Sex sucks. It's raw and uncomfortable even though he is gentle and slow. He suggests I go on top so that I can control the rhythm, and it still hurts. No matter how much I rock and writhe and moan, he never cums. It still hurts, and I realize in one horrific flash that everyone has probably been lying to me my entire life. Sex is a conspiracy. A big, fat, horrible lie that everyone pretends is great and wonderful and fun just to trick people into procreation. Damn those *American Pie* movies. This isn't the Holy Grail of teenagedom. This is *The Emperor's New Clothes*.

A week goes by and it's time for Adam to leave for Wyoming. I'm going to miss his arms and his poems and his laugh, but I am surprised by how relieved I am that I can stop worrying about how to make sex good for a little while.

chapter twelve

EDUCATION SUCKS

It's the first day of CitySemester and we're gathered around for orientation. Virgil, the program director, talks like his brain is dancing, sending out giddy oom-pah synapse snaps to every other part of his body. He is a red-bearded giant. His arms shoot out, fingers splayed, as he announces, "This—*right here*—a room of thirty people with thirty completely unique *universes* of perspective—is an organism through which we can discover things about the world, about each other, and about ourselves. Things that we don't know. Things that we don't even *know* that we don't know! Which reminds me, are there any questions?"

A prim girl from Texas raises her hand. "Can you tell us about the grading process?"

Virgil smiles knowingly. "Well, we don't have any grades. We do holistic written evaluations. "

Before I have a chance to ask a follow-up question, Virgil starts explaining our first trip. "We're going to see a fantastic piece of experimental theater, truly innovative, and I want everyone to get me a thorough, thoughtful reflection by the weekend."

Texas's hand shoots up. "Page minimum?"

Virgil shrugs. "Whatever you think."

She furrows her brow and writes a big question mark in her assignment pad next to the project title. She underlines it and taps her pen anxiously while Virgil starts to talk about theater as a means of cultural communication.

I can't help myself—I have to know. "So, I know there's no minimum, but could you give us a page *estimate*?"

Virgil chuckles. "Don't worry about it. Write however many pages it takes for you to finish your thought."

A tall shaggy kid asks, "But what if our thought only takes up, like, one paragraph?"

"Then I bet it's a very potent thought. I look forward to reading it."

"What if it's only a sentence?"

"I'll take an honest sentence over a recycled novel any day," says Virgil, adding, "though I certainly hope you give yourself credit for more than a sentence's worth of reflection."

That night, thirty juniors from around the globe, all of us giddy with get-to-know-you jitters, pile onto the subway to go see the show. My mother has always hated the subway.

"Stand behind the yellow line," she used to warn when I was a little girl.

"Ma, I am behind the yellow line."

"But you're not braced behind a handrail or a column. Someone could just toss you into the track if they wanted to."

"That's silly."

"Subways are dangerous. They're the Ebola virus of transportation."

"What?!"

"Behind the yellow line."

When CitySemester reaches 14th Street everyone pours out, but I am sucked backwards by a churning crowd of rush hour commuters. I reach the door just as it closes. In a panic, I squeeze my way to the window, pounding on the glass to no avail. Virgil turns to me calmly from outside the subway car, smiles, and points toward the ceiling as if to say, "Meet you up there." I feel my heart pound as the subway lurches forward into the darkness of subterranean New York. I'm all alone. Lost on the big bad subway. *Shit.*

Across from me I see an eight-year-old sitting by himself reading *Harry Potter*, and as we speed along I realize that if he can navigate the subway, so can I. *Pull it together.* This is merely an unexpected detour, and all I have to do is work my way back.

I get off the subway at the next stop and ask a dozen different people to confirm that the train uptown does indeed lead back to where I came from. As I wait for my train, I stare down cautiously at the yellow line. Slowly, warily, keeping my weight on my back leg, I creep my toe forward, inch by inch. I look over my shoulder to make sure that no one is lurking, waiting to hurl me into the tracks. And then I take two big steps right past the yellow line.

I make my way back to 14th Street and emerge from the subway into the lights of the city—the bustling crowds, the hum of traffic, the smell of warm roasted peanuts, the little glints of silver in the pavement below. I find my way to the theater just in time for the show. New York City is mine.

We are standing in a dark empty room in a big under-
ground New York City theater. A white tarp suspended above
us is illuminated by soft lights, and the pitter-patter of sweet
plinking notes descends from all around as splotches of neon
paint land on the canopy above. They splash and drip, roll
and blend, pooling together to form a tie-dye canvas on the
ceiling. It billows and trembles. Suddenly, a woman rips
through with a CRASH on a bungee cord, plucks up a shrieking audience member, and returns back from whence she
came amidst a swirl of smoke and confetti.

Drums pound and the canvas shreds to reveal the rest of
the cavernous room, which echoes with salsa drums. A
vibrant jungle of acrobats begins to weave through the crowd,
flying and whooping. The audience is herded toward a single
sweaty body writhing in a smoky cocoon of red-orange light.
A steamy dream. We part to make way for rolling pillars, each
supporting a dozen dancers stomping and shouting in explosive synchronicity as golden flecks pepper the air. Trumpets
blare and a torrent of water gushes forth from above, dousing
the dancers, who pound the ground with even more passion
and precision. It's surreal.

By the end of the show, even the dainty belle from Texas in
the white cable-knit sweater vest has given herself over to the
beat, swaying her hips daintily, while some more adventur-
ous classmates, at the encouragement of the cast, strip off
extraneous pieces of clothing and bounce jubilantly in
puddles of color and water, their flailing limbs illuminated
in choppy strobes of light. They look pretty ridiculous, my

invisible camera observes, but they also look like they're having a whole lot of fun. Still, I don't jump into the middle of the throng. It's cold outside and I have on my fancy dry-clean-only theater shirt and I don't want to get wet and I'm not going to make an ass of myself in front of everyone on the first day.

A tropical blue mist envelops the crowd. The waterfall erupts again. The music pounds and the colors flash and when I feel the warm hand of one of the dancers pulling me toward him, finally I just say, "Fuck it." Who cares? I shut off the camera. I am alone. For twenty glorious seconds, I jump and wiggle and wave, shrieking and shaking out my hair and getting completely drenched before the water is turned off and the lights are turned on and everyone is herded into the startlingly plain fluorescence of the lobby.

This is not your average high school afternoon.

CitySemester classes are fantastically messy, and we don't have to constantly rein ourselves in to keep on track for AP exams. If we're talking about urban planning in Central Park and want to go off on a tangent about graffiti and Basquiat, we can. If we're discussing tense culture clashes in the bloody Five Points district in the 1800s and want to talk about how it's being portrayed in the new Scorsese movie, we do. And then we go see the movie and visit the places where it was shot and try to get an interview with the screenwriter. It's amazing.

In our first official literature section, I come armed with my underlined, highlighted copy of *Gatsby* and am prepared to kick discussion ass. Everyone sits around the table expectantly as Virgil plops down in his chair and leans forward.

"So?" He scratches his beard thoughtfully. "What do we think?"

For a moment, nobody speaks. Then Texas raises her hand. "Well, I was struck by the symbolism of the Valley of Ashes. Like how Fitzgerald shows that the morals of the 1920s are decaying."

Dammit. That's what I was going to say.

"Okay, great. And?"

"And," Texas rifles through her notes, "the ashes represent the downside of . . . excess? It foreshadows the Depression and stuff."

"And what do you *personally* think about that?" Virgil probes.

Texas stares blankly. She twirls her pencil and chews her bottom lip, eyeing Virgil suspiciously. " . . . Is this gonna be on the test?"

Virgil dashes to the whiteboard and draws a picture of two stick figures at either end. "This," he says, pointing to the figure on the left, "is the author, the artist." He walks to the other side of the board. "Now this is *you*—the reader, the listener." He doodles a giant pair of glasses onto the stick person. "And these are your 'perspective lenses.' They are colored by every part of your life: your parents, your friends, the culture and time you grew up in. Maybe you have six little sisters, maybe you're a Buddhist, maybe you were bitten by a Dalmatian when you were four years old. All of these things play a part in forming your own unique perspective. And this is where it gets exciting!"

Virgil leaps toward the center of the board and draws a book. "Once an artist puts his work into the public sphere, it takes on a life of its own. And no matter how many thousands of people encounter it over the centuries, by reading it through your own *completely unique* lens, you are creating a new conceptual marriage that has never existed before in the history of the world!" He encircles the book in a manic triple scribble. "And then you might create your *own* art, which will shade the lenses of *future* artists, and on and on . . . " He clutches his hands to his head. "Just imagine! Your children's children's children might hear something in Mozart or da Vinci or Fitzgerald that even the artists themselves didn't know, could never have *conceived* of at the time. Something that was waiting five hundred years to be heard!"

He settles back into his chair and leans toward us with saucer eyes and the earnest reverence of a magician incanting the final lines of his most powerful spell. "Potent writing, potent art, potent *ideas*," he says, "will travel. Will traverse continents and cultures, transcend generations in an endless chain of inspiration, of opportunity for change. Ideas are shape shifters, rabble-rousers, communal muses, evolving conversations. They are . . . the living whisper."

Texas, who has been scribbling down frantic notes, asks if any of *this* is going to be on the test.

"Regurgitating things that other people have said only proves to me that you have the capacity of a moderately intelligent parakeet. You guys are better than that. Tell me what you think. Show me how you can apply what you've learned. Go start some living whispers."

And class ends.

I go to my computer to write my reflection on the previous evening's performance and decide I need to call Virgil's bluff.

Hannah. De La Guarda performance.

I want to believe in dancing for the hell of it
And getting real messy before you get clean.
Laughing through sorrow and lusting toward light
And making guacamole naked.

Sex.
Seh-eh-ex.
Passion, panting, two sets of limbs and a single pulse.
One encompassing one encompassing everything.
Rawness.
Ringlets ravaged.
Toes curled.
Drums pound
Trumpets sound
While the branches bow at our whim
And the oceans rumble
And the mountains crumble
And the earth's crust cracks in our bliss.
Leaving nothing but us
Intertwined amidst a stark and starry sky
Pulsing with white heat.

I lust after emotions.
My own are rust or golden glistening. And others?

Others have new colors and nestled within them are
    pieces of me.
I am mad with want of them.
I want soulful blue and moody orange and harlot gray.
I want to wrap myself in a weightless shroud of
    shreds of myself
So maybe then I'd feel whole.
Gain control. Lifelessness of lazy Sundays
    takes a toll till sometimes—
Sometimes I am shattered and desperate
Clinging to scraps of the colors of others.
I need a rainbow.

When I finish I print it out and drop it in Virgil's box. When it is returned later that week, I am surprised to find that there is not a trace of red pen. Instead, the only writing is a happy purple scribble at the bottom that reads, "Fascinating. Let's talk." But it isn't an ominous, see-me-after-class "Let's talk." I think he might actually want to just talk.

And we talk. We talk about my use of color and our favorite Coltrane albums and what he learned about life from coaching high school soccer. Virgil asks me about my writing process, about what I want to learn and where I want to improve. I read through my weekly holistic written evaluation and realize that for all the dozens of A's and B's I've received at Danforth, nobody but Ms. Lynn ever once bothered to take me aside and give me any further feedback. It feels good to be more than just a list of letters on a transcript.

At CitySemester, we volunteer at soup kitchens and day-care centers and talk with the homeless people I used to pretend not to see on my way to SoHo for shopping trips with the Great Eight. I feel ashamed for passing them by. They are good people. They're funny and smart, gentle and artistic, bursting with so many stories that I never thought to ask about. So many labels that I never thought to question. Virgil reminds us that nothing is simply what it seems, and the more we learn about New York City history, the more stories seem to spring up around every corner. I wander down Wall Street and think about how, three hundred years ago, it actually was a wall, built by the New Amsterdam colony to keep out Native Americans. I think about the myth of the American Dream as we visit the tenement museum, straining our eyes in the dark, cramped, crumbling rooms that used to house twelve immigrants at a time, each cot shared by three different people in rotating shifts.

Nowhere are culturally rich stories more abundant than in our exploration of the Brooklyn Bridge. We trace the development of suspension bridges through architectural history, and then we examine the blueprints to calculate the load-bearing force and tensile strength of the physical structure. We see paintings inspired by the bridge and read interviews with the workers who toiled away in the caissons. We watch how steel tension cables are spun. We read poetry about the bridge—stanzas about "waves of iron," sister cities and silver parapets. Everything is related, intricately interwoven instead of disconnected, compartmentalized, and squashed into multiple-choice Scantron wastelands like all of my classes at Danforth.

I decide that for my Brooklyn Bridge reflection I'm going to write a song. At least a million separate times after I decide it's a good idea, I'm sure it is actually the worst idea I've ever had. I don't know the right chords and my fingering is clumsy and the lyrics are trite, but a part of me knows that if I don't do it now I'll never forgive myself. Writing is hard. I feel like I'm vanquishing massive dragons of self-doubt at every turn—*you suck, what an awful idea, god, that's stupid. How can you even imagine people are ever going to want to listen to this?*

I talk with Virgil a lot about writing. He encourages me not to abandon little wisps of ideas just because they aren't fully formed yet, to give silly images a chance. My stupid sentence about taxi cabs leads to an interesting verse about the rhythm of the city, my stupid D chord evolves into a nice simple melody, and before I know it, I'm sitting in front of my friends on presentation day with a full set of lyrics and a guitar in my hand. I steel myself for the tightness in my throat, the wobbly knees, but as I strum the first chord of the first real song that I ever actually let myself finish, I feel more proud of this than of all the A papers I've written in my entire life. I watch my friends and my teachers, their smiles of encouragement urging me on, and I sing with confidence. And now, every time I watch a movie or see a postcard featuring the bridge, I carry a secret smile, because I know that in some small way, I have lent my very own whisper to its existence. And that whisper has a killer, thumpin' bass line.

After about two months, a very strange thing happens. Everyone starts to wear pajamas to class. This might not sound like a revolution or a revelation or anything, but coming from a place where people wake up an extra hour and a half early just to straighten, conceal, highlight, and moisturize themselves to polished perfection, it's pretty startling to see an entire classroom populated with bed head and residue from last night's pimple cream. Spending twenty-four hours a day with each other on the train and in the theater and discussing art exhibitions and making morning pancakes makes it increasingly difficult to hide much of anything. Farts and snorts and temper tantrums and secret obsessions with Superman slowly bubble to the surface in a refreshing burst of reality. It feels really, really good.

I reward myself by abandoning my diet entirely. I eat Brooklyn pizza, delight in Chinatown *dim sum*, and scarf down hot dogs with all the toppings on the Coney Island boardwalk. After depriving myself of dessert for the better part of two years, New York City cheesecake is the closest my taste buds have ever come to heaven. I buy it at the train station on Saturdays to reward myself after a long week. Then on Wednesdays I'm buying two fat wedges at a time to save some for later. CitySemester work is rewarding, but it's stressful nonetheless, and in a few weeks my pants are cutting a blubbery crease into my hips. I feel disgusting again. *What was I thinking? How could I have let myself slip so far?* I'm despicable, unfixable, and I will never learn. I run until I am nauseous. I eat only baby food and carrot sticks for four days. I binge until I'm about to burst, then purge until my eyes are so clouded with tears I can't see and my throat is coated in fire. I am loathsome. But I can change. I put on my running shoes, make myself promises, and it begins again.

After a few weeks of this, coupled with the intense CitySemester travel schedule, my stomach decides to revolt. I start throwing up things I never intended to. I have searing pains no matter what I eat and cramps so crippling they force me to take taxis up the hill from the train station instead of walking with the group. It gets so bad that they send me home. I see doctors. They all ask me if I have allergies, if I drink or smoke. They do blood tests.

"Is there anything else you want to tell me?" they ask.

How about that I'm such a disgusting, out-of-control cow that I ate myself sick? I don't think so. I hope they'll discover some rare thyroid condition or crazy virus that can account for my insatiable appetite, but nobody finds anything. They put me on a strict diet of applesauce and rice, which means maybe now I'll lose all the stupid weight. But being at home alone in the house is boring and depressing. I'm lonely and bloated. One evening, I find myself kneeling in front of the refrigerator, eating slice after slice after slice of an enormous, sickeningly sweet honey baked ham. I am *inhaling* ham. I eat and I eat until I punch myself in the arm hard, *hard*, because it's what I deserve.

The doctors prescribe pills to coat my stomach and chalk my pain up to a strange gastrointestinal flare-up. Eventually, I am well enough to return. When I walk back into my room, I find every surface covered with little index cards that say things like, "We missed your laugh!" and "We missed all your comments in Virgil's class!" I am taken aback.

Television convinced me long ago that I had no real friends. The *Dawson's Creek*, *90210*, and *Friends* friends all went on vacation together and knew each other's most intimate secrets and threw each other lavishly themed surprise parties. Nobody has ever, ever thrown me a surprise party (not counting my eighth-grade "surprise, there's no party" party, for which Genevieve and all of her cronies RSVPed and then failed to show up). I am pretty sure this means I'm a friendship failure. But I look around at these index cards, these little squares of real affection and genuine compassion, and I feel absolutely appreciated and loved. By real friends. I know it would be cheesy to cry, but after being holed up in my house all alone for so many days, convinced I was a complete fuck-up, it means a lot to me. I feel wanted. And not the kind of lunch table inclusion where you know you could be the victim of a massive backstabbing attack as soon as you leave the table.

"Thanks a lot, you guys."

"You're back!" one of my roommates says, jumping up from her bed to embrace me.

The others run to join us. "Our room was so empty without all your stuff spilling out of the closet!"

"Yeah, we missed you."

I'm home.

We are preparing our *The Things They Carried* project, inspired by an essay from Tim O'Brien's book that describes American soldiers in the Vietnam War through their personal items and memories. Everyone is pretty nervous about it. Sure, it might be okay to show everyone your crazy morning hair, but that's only the tip of the iceberg—what if they knew about all the craziness underneath? We all whine and procrastinate until the night before, as usual, when my roommates and I sit on our beds, staring at the laptops in our laps with concern.

The statuesque South African girl I've admired all semester

comes in, also tearing her hair out, and we commiserate. After two more hours of popcorn and furious typing, she raises her long, lovely arms in a congratulatory stretch and announces, "I think I'm ready."

She reads us a story about a photograph she carries that her mother took. Her mother has cancer. We didn't know. She talks about playing silly games with her sister by the side of a river, about feeling like as much of an outsider in America as she does in South Africa, about grief and anger and jealousy for all the people whose parents aren't "broken." Her words flow out like long violin strokes, resonating with soft simplicity. And when she's finished, our eyes are wet.

"That was beautiful."

"You don't think I should take out the part about the—"

"Don't change a thing."

And for the first time in my life, I want nothing more than to tell them. To be heard. Maybe if I just say it, expose it to the light, my secret shame will lose some of its power and shrivel up and one day maybe even blow away. I am tired of pretending. If I wait to write it down I might lose the nerve.

I swallow. "I think I have a problem." *Shut the fuck up, you fat lazy whore. You make yourself miserable with your own disgusting—*

"I—I'm really fucked up with food," I stammer.

There it is. I said it. I said it, and I can't take it back. I am overcome by a powerful sense of relief. They hug me. I breathe.

We hear the last reading. We take our last subway ride. We listen to Virgil's last acrobatic literary lecture. And as quickly as it arrived, CitySemester disappears from my life and becomes a memory, a whisper, leaving behind nothing more than my writing portfolio to remind me. Mom and Dad help me move back into my room at home, and I sit on my bed surrounded by bags of dirty laundry. I glance at my massive AP summer reading list and cannot help but wish I could press rewind.

chapter thirteen

HOME SUCKS

After the freedom of CitySemester, being at home makes me even more claustrophobic than living in the tour bus four years earlier. I've gone from setting my own schedule and planning solo expeditions through the largest city in the United States to being (according to my mother) completely incapable of even deciding which way to drive to the post office.

"You're taking Route *Nine*?" Mom balks. "Eighty-four will get you there in half the time, and you'll miss rush hour! Most automobile deaths happen between five and—"

My mother wants to know where I'm going, when I'm going, and with whom, and also why I haven't taken out the garbage yet. She bursts into my room at all hours demanding to know all sorts of everything. She's a tornado of nagging, and more often than not, I am caught in her path. We always end up screaming at each other. I lock my door and she threatens to take off the hinges.

"I dare you," I shout.

My father, who has been silent until now, cautions, "Sweetie, I don't suggest you ever dare your mother."

The next morning I wake up with no door. I snap at her for being such an evil, controlling bitch and, small as she is, she wrestles me into the shower with all of my clothes on and turns on the cold water. My mother is insane. My father never listens, only lectures, because he is always, *always* right, and if you don't listen to him, you're being an impatient *child*. I can't stand the sight of him gorging himself on pastries. Sam has become an excellent jazz pianist, and every time I hear him playing complicated melodies, I secretly wish I could snap off his little prodigy fingers because it reminds me of how much of a fake, slacker musician I am.

The only good thing about summer is that Adam is coming back. I have missed him. The poems and letters and sand dollars he sends me fill a little box in my bookshelf, and every time I look at it, I cannot help thinking I am the luckiest girl in the world. He lands in New York on a Tuesday afternoon, drives straight to my house, and doesn't move out for the rest of the summer. He gets a job at the coffee shop down the street from where I waitress and we read each other books, hang out with the hippies, and smoke pot in the tree house.

"I love your family," he says one evening as we sip pomegranate tea in the treetops.

"Are you nuts?"

"You should appreciate them, babe. They're really cool."

I sip my tea and take the joint. "You're high."

"I'm also right."

"And high."

He stretches his arms out and stands up. "C'mon, let's go play Scrabble with them."

180

"What?!"

He begins to climb down the ladder. "It'll be fun!"

I haven't been high around my family before, and by the time I scramble down the ladder Adam is already chatting with my mother in the kitchen and setting up the Scrabble board. Amelia inspects the tiles Adam dumps onto the table, and my invisible camera notes how Amelia has these amazingly intricate swirls on the fleshy part of her fingers—little black fingerprints.

We play Scrabble. My mother is beautiful and witty, and even when she is crass, I know she's just trying to make us laugh. Every time it is my father's turn, he takes a loooong pause. This usually drives me crazy, but tonight I watch the way he sticks his tongue out a bit like a little boy putting together a model car, considering, crafting. I remember how when I was afraid to go to the bathroom at night as a kid, he bought glow-in-the-dark paint and made all the walls into an undersea wonderland, with dolphins darting to and fro behind the sink, big silly clown fish flanking the towel racks, and curly swirly sea anemones crowding every inch of the ceiling. It was like a secret nighttime world. I wasn't afraid after that. Sam has become a handsome young man—thoughtful, funny, wise. I'm proud of him. I watch my family. I love them.

I love Adam. Over the course of the summer we fix the terrible sex, which turns out to have been the result of not enough lubrication, not enough communication, and the fact that I am severely allergic to the brand of condoms we've been using. We buy K-Y Jelly and a colorful assortment of new types of condoms and figure things out. I admit that shaving my pubic hair into the neat thin strip that everybody seems to expect is a total fucking nightmare, because it always results in painful little red ingrown bumps. He tells me that I should stop doing it because he loves me for me, not for my pubic hair.

"Nobody ever complained the grass was too high at Disney World," he kids.

I toss a pillow at him playfully. "Oh, and you have to cut your fingernails," I tell him. "They're scratchy."

"Sorry, baby. Mmm, that reminds me, though. Teeth and blow jobs, not such a good pair."

"Well, I don't know what the hell to do down there. You're the penis expert. I wish you would just tell me what you like."

"You're right. I'll tell you all about it if you promise to show me how to make you cum when I go down on you. And never squeeze my balls like that again. Seriously. They're sensitive."

"Well, so are my breasts," I inform him. "They're not—"

"Doorknobs?" He falls back into the pillows laughing and I straddle his chest, pinning his arms above his head with my hands.

"Who told you about that?"

"Baby, I think it's adorable. I love that story!"

"I know, I know, hilaaarious . . . who told you?"

He sits up and wraps his arms around my waist, nuzzling my sternum with his nose and then leaning in to kiss my left nipple lightly. "I don't know. I think that blondie friend of yours from photo—back when she was always trying to convince me you were crazy."

"What?"

"Ahh, your breasts are amazin—"

"Cashmere told you I was crazy?"

182

"Oh, yeah, all the time," he says into my breast, swirling his tongue around.

I push his head away. "And what did you say?"

He's still staring at my breasts.

"Hello?" I snap my fingers in front of his face.

He shakes his head. "What?"

I pull the sheet up toward my neck. "What did you say when she told you I was crazy?"

He grins. "Well, I told her you were brilliant and creative and that I had a huge crush on you . . . and that you had a fantastic rack."

"You cretin!"

We laugh and kiss and make love, and before we know it it's time for Adam to leave for college. All the way across the country. We promise everything will be the same when he gets back for Christmas break. With Adam gone, I remember what it's like when my family isn't having nice Scrabble moments. My mother sits at the kitchen table with her head in her hands, surrounded by bills, deciding which ones we can afford to pay. Finances are especially tight this summer, and college looms just over the horizon. The car broke down again and we can't afford to fix it. My mother is horrible to my father. He is horrible right back. School cannot start soon enough.

I can count on one hand the number of times I've heard my Dad raise his voice, but when it does happen, it's scary. The power has been turned off and my mother screams something about albums and responsibilities and IBM, and Dad just snaps.

"If you weren't such a selfish little bitch, if you had even an *ounce* of encouragement in you instead of just *mineminemine*—"

"Look at me. Have you even *looked* at me lately? I could leave you *tomorrow* and marry a millionaire by next week."

"Shutupshutupshutup!" I shout from my bedroom.

Mom never cries, but I can tell when she wants to. "I didn't want this. I never wanted this. This isn't what you promised me."

Later, when things have settled down, I ask Mom what she meant by IBM.

"Your father turned down a job there," she tells me bitterly. "We could have paid off the mortgage and the car loans within a year. It was ten times what he makes now, but he said he couldn't compromise his 'creative integrity.'" She shakes her head. "Just what we need, *another* fucking album nobody's going to buy."

My father is irresponsible, and I will never forgive him. I decide two more things. First, I'm going to be rich. I will buy my parents a house so my mother can stop hating her life. I don't care if Cashmere's mother drinks herself to sleep and her father is cheating on her with some exotic dancer. At least they don't have to worry about the electricity being turned off. At least their kitchen counter isn't covered with monkey shit. My second decision is that I'm moving into the dorms. I need to get away. The summer comes to a close and I return to Danforth for my final year. Senior year. Round four.

chapter fourteen

COLLEGE SUCKS

"Quiet. Quiet!" a harried secretary shouts at the senior class. "This is *your* future, people, not mine! QUIET!"

The chatter settles as a hundred thick blue binders get passed out.

"This," the secretary announces, holding one of the binders above her head with such reverence you'd think she were hefting the Ten Commandments, "is your *college compendium*. Inside you'll find application timetables, sample essays, everything you'll need to apply to college, including . . . " she flips to the back, "the famous *admit rubric*."

She pauses for effect. Julian takes the opportunity to let out an enormous belch. We all break into riotous laughter as the secretary scurries back and forth trying to get everyone under control. Mrs. Berman, the college counselor, suddenly appears and we all shut up. You don't mess around with Mrs. Berman. Everyone knows that a phone call from her can make or break a placement. She wears bold jewel tones and gives big hugs, and she is notoriously ruthless about making sure that her "babies" get into the colleges of their dreams.

"These rubrics," she declares cheerily, thumbing through dozens of pages of graphy things covered in colored dots, "contain hundreds of destinies, thousands of hours of work and dedication. Each page represents a different school, and each dot, a student who applied there. Weighted GPAs and SAT scores run along the horizontal and vertical axes. A red dot means a rejection. Yellow is waitlist. Green means they got in." She snaps the binder closed. "One day soon, each of you will become happy little dots, and it's my job to make sure that you all turn out green."

I flip through the pages and wonder which dots correspond to whom. Some of them are obvious, like the genius valedictorian with perfect SATs who got into Harvard; her green dot is balanced on the top right corner of the Harvard graph. Or the girl who went to Harvard the next year, whose spot (everyone said) had been purchased by her father. Her green dot stands out all the way at the bottom of the graph in the lower left corner. Two green dots on opposite corners, separated by a sea of red. No yellow. Apparently Harvard doesn't need to waitlist.

Mrs. Berman explains that this semester is the most crucial of our entire lives. "Everything you've ever done in high school has been leading up to this, kiddos, so now is *not* the time to start suffering from senioritis. This year is going to be the toughest admissions season we've ever seen. Your entire future depends on the next few months. If you want me to work hard for you, you eat, sleep, and breathe college applications from now on."

Yeesh.

I cringe at the thought of rededicating myself to the mindless drudgery of test-test-test-paper after my enlightening time at CitySemester. School doesn't have to *be* like this! Classes can be funny and engaging and surprising and *relevant*, instead of the endlessly unsatisfying game of "guess what this teacher wants to hear." Rinse, repeat. But it seems that if I want all of my hard work over the past three years to count for anything, if I want to get into a good college where I'll find people like me, if I want to save my parents from retiring into a cardboard shantytown, I'm going to have to buckle down.

Mac and I are elected as cochairs, the top positions in student government, presiding over Morning Meeting and heading up the Executive and Disciplinary Committees. I'm president of the drama society. I'm in more AP classes than I can keep in my head. Jazz band. The musical. By the second week of school, my life has become one endless tunnel of over-scheduled overachievement, with the only small speck of distant light being an early acceptance letter from some dream school come December.

I haven't missed much being away from the Great Eight— a few break-ups, make-outs, make-ups, nothing new. But none of the usual drama could ever compare to the torrent of hysteria that overtakes the lunch table when college applications begin to loom large. The Ivy League is the new designer purse, except the Ivy League is better than any purse. It's not the type of label that any bimbo with Daddy's credit card can buy. It's an authentic, vintage, limited edition *life* label. And if you don't get one, you might as well die.

"Ohmigod," squeals Teagan. "I visited Princeton this weekend, and I'm, like, in love. I swear to God, if I don't get in I'll, like, slit my wrists."

All of the girls assure her that she is *such* an amazing applicant, there is no reason why the admissions reps will not *absolutely* fall *completely* love with her. Teagan pops a piece of gum in her mouth and dashes off to the bathroom for a minute. The girls all count to ten in their heads.

Cashmere strikes first. "Princeton would accept my *dog* before they would accept her."

"Well, I heard she has connections," says a B knowingly.

"Connections can't convince an *Ivy* to take the girl who thought Polonius told Ophelia she speaks 'like a green girl' because she makes him 'like, nauseous.' I mean, come on, you read that *Hamlet* paper of hers in class yesterday," Cashmere scoffs. "She's a joke! She's always been a joke!"

"Yeah, I know, but she's totally gonna play the minority card," another B chimes in.

The group pauses in consideration. Tension settles over the table as the girls consider the magnitude of Teagan Delgado's competitive edge: a bilingual heiress with a double Princeton legacy and United Nations connections. What's a white girl from Westchester to do? Suddenly, Cashmere gasps, grinning as if she has just discovered a two-for-one Jimmy Choo sale. With elation, she divulges her juicy story.

"Well, *my* mother heard from my SAT tutor, who works with *Teagan's* SAT tutor, that her diagnostics were bad. Like, really, really bad. Like, she's barely breaking a 500. She's—"

Two Bs glare at Cashmere, indicating the return of their ethnically fortunate opponent. The girls giggle with satisfaction as Teagan saunters back to the table, a fresh layer of mascara upon her long lashes.

"Whatcha talkin' about?"

"Oh, nothin' that'll amount to much," Cashmere tells her with a wicked grin.

"Hey, anybody want to tour UPenn with me next weekend?" a B asks.

"Eiw," says Cashmere. "I mean—no, thanks."

"Where even is that, like, Vermont?" Teagan asks.

Cashmere rolls her eyes, "You're lucky you're a legacy, Tea." She turns. "And, seriously, eiw."

"UPenn is an Ivy!"

"Barely."

"Where are you applying, Hannz?"

I take a bite of lettuce. "I'm not sure yet."

"Well, maybe you can go wherever Adam is. Where is he, anyway, like, Colorado or something?" Teagan smiles at me generously. "I hear you can really stretch a buck there."

"And with all the hiking and stuff, you would totally lose the weight!" Cashmere adds.

I clear my tray and walk down the steps of the dining hall. I don't come back. Ever.

College tours are overwhelmingly similar. Every place has *stellar* academics, an *amazing* curriculum, *fantastic* classes. Everything runs together into a big mush of "diversity," "research opportunities," and "global outlook." After the seventh campus tour, I start to feel like I am living in an infomercial.

Then I visit Yale.

There is nothing particularly special about the Yale tour. The buildings are old and hallowed like at Harvard. The main street is small but quaint like at Brown. The campus green bustles like at Princeton. But then we go to the information session. A well-spoken man in a well-pressed suit does the cursory overview of statistics and then starts taking questions. Someone asks, "What makes a Yalie?" The same question has been asked by some nervous parent at every other college I've visited so far, but this time, instead of rattling off pat answers like "intellectual curiosity," he simply stretches his arms as if dangling a set of golden keys, casually rotating his wrists as he turns over possible answers in his head.

"I have to be honest," he says with an easy smile. "We could kill off our entire freshman class and fill every single spot with statistically identical applicants from the waitlist." He pauses. "We could do that four or five times over. Yale is about so much more than numbers."

Did this guy really just describe the strength of the applicant pool with a genocide analogy? Is that even okay? I am disturbed by how disturbing this is, but even more disturbed by how strangely alluring I find it. It seems that Yale has a special system, an ancient secret, an invisible measure of excellence too precise to be detected by the crudely calibrated standardized tests used on the masses. Yale senses a rare essence that elevates their admits beyond the elementary realm of GPAs and colored dots on a graph somewhere. Yalies cannot be encapsulated by simple green dots—they are so much more than that. They are green *spheres*. If what my parents have told me my whole life about being special is true—if all of the suckiness I'm going through with AP classes and late nights of homework and dealing with administration isn't a colossal waste of time—if I'm ever going to be rich and happy and be the best I can be—I must get into Yale. I must.

At the first college meeting with Mrs. Berman and my parents, we start laying out battle tactics: safeties, targets, and reaches, all sorted by region and affordability and difficulty. I ask her about Yale. She nods with satisfied certainty.

"It would be perfect for you. Absolutely perfect." But she is quick to temper my enthusiasm. "You must remember it's a reach, though. A big reach." She turns to my parents. "This year, admission is going to be tougher than ever, so we'll need solid targets and safeties."

My dad stares out the window. "I don't know, honey bunny. I really liked Vassar. Remember that long tree branch? Wasn't that amazing? I think they said it was the longest unsupported tree branch in the entire world."

"Dad, I'm not going to a school because of a long tree branch! This is my *future!*"

"Everybody was so nice there."

My parents just don't get it. They don't know what it's been like to have Great Eighters watching your every move. They don't understand what a crushing defeat it would be to go to an average school after all my years of striving to be something more. I'm going to Yale. I apply Early Action. It's the perfect decision—the only decision. My application must be flawless.

I visit my parents to get help with the Yale financial aid forms. My mother is browsing through my résumé when she asks, "So what stops you from saying you were the president of the basketball team? Are they going to call and check?"

"I don't know, Mom. Basketball teams have captains, not presidents."

"Then we should say you were captain!"

"Mom, *please!*" I snap, not amused.

"And write down how you speak Yiddish, too. There's no way they'll have an interviewer who speaks Yiddish, so they can't prove that you don't."

"That's a terrible idea!"

"Well, fine. I was just trying to be helpful."

"I have always said," Dad mumbles through bites of a chicken wing, "that you should be recording an application essay in *song* form."

Mom smacks the table. "Yes! Brilliant. And Amelia can be in it. She can be the star—"

"I'm the star!" I scream. "I am the star of my own college application, and I don't need to lie or sing songs or wave around a fucking monkey. I'm good enough to get in on my own!"

Dad puts down the chicken wing sheepishly. "We know that, sweetie. We were just joking. You seem really stressed about this, and we thought it would be funny—"

"Yeah, well, if you knew anything about this bullshit process, you'd know that nothing about it is funny."

Rumor has it that Teagan's mother has hired a private college advisor who charges thirty thousand dollars and guarantees Ivy acceptance or your money back. Parents scramble to make sure applications are beyond perfect. They pull strings to get recommendations from governors and senators. They take prominent alumni out to dinner at five-star restaurants. And I hear that Dot is arranging a huge charity fashion gala so that Cashmere can take credit for it on her resume. It's Ivy or die.

In the dorms, the coin of the realm is either weed or Adderall, depending on how productive you feel like being.

Weed is for those "fuck it" days when all you want to do is eat gummy worms down by the river. Adderall is for when you're in business mode. My Yale application is due in a few weeks and I'm up to six hours of homework a night, so I am in full-on business mode. I don't even have time to long for the freedom of CitySemester anymore.

Adderall is a little pill that comes in a variety of shapes and colors depending on the dosage—thirty milligrams is a prize, but even the little round five milligram pills can get you through a four-page paper. It's prescribed to help people with ADHD to focus, but in the dorm it's used for pulling insane all-nighters. Maybe it's the placebo effect, but somehow the entire world shuts the fuck up once you're in the Adderall zone. You feel speedy and heady and driven. *Write. Write it.* The hours tick by, and you just keep zooming down the track like you are soldered to the front of a steam engine. You speedspeedspeed ahead until you look back and the whole thing's done.

You hardly have time to celebrate, though, because by that time it's 6 AM and you've been up all night, so your eyes twitch and your brain melts and sometimes you start to get paranoid. *Did you hear that? Was someone looking in my window?* If you make the mistake of popping too many pills late at night or on an empty stomach, you end up rocking in your bed unproductively, teeth chattering, eyes pried open by jolts of anxiety. It's not pleasant, but if you're careful with the dosage, Adderall can make the difference between writing one paper in a night or three. Even though I don't sit with them at lunch, I still hear Great Eighters chatting before class about our alleged Ivy League competitors: junior Olympians, published authors, quadrilingual science fair champions. If I don't write three papers tonight, I might as well drop out and join the circus right now.

The kids to whom the Adderall is prescribed are high status in the dorm. Even if they're not your friends, you do favors for them—share your notes, lend them clothing—all in the hope that when you're really desperate for some poppable focus they will be willing to share. But during midterms and finals, not even friendship can counteract high demand, and prices soar as high as eight bucks per pill.

An added benefit to taking Adderall is that it suppresses appetite. I watch Luna's younger sister—a lovely, plump, happy artist—waste away into a skeleton with dark circles under her eyes within half a semester of getting diagnosed with ADHD. She stops painting. She gets snappy with friends and flakes out on coffee dates and stops chatting in the common room. One afternoon she passes out in gym class. All the girls in the dorm hold a mini intervention to tell her that we're worried, that she hasn't been herself lately. She tells us we're crazy.

"Look at you! You're wasting away!" her roommate insists, clearly upset.

"Fine," she agrees reluctantly. "I guess I could cut back a little bit on weekends."

"We're here to support you, babe," I say, giving her a big hug.

Another Ivy hopeful corners her as the girls disperse. "Hey . . . can I get dibs on your leftover weekend pills?"

But Adderall is hardly everyone's drug of choice. Weed is popular, and even more colorful things usually pour in after weekends spent at home raiding Mommy's medicine cabinet.

Lots of girls steal Ambien, a sleeping pill that'll knock you for a hallucinogenic loop if you fight the sleepiness and stay awake long enough to break into the trippiness. One girl gets handfuls of Vicodin from her equestrian mother; she and her roommates take enough to medicate a horse, put on comfy pajamas, draw the curtains, and sit four abreast watching *Sex and the City* for two days straight.

Once in a while the dorm community gets a big score. Julian moves into the dorms after extensive feuding with his parents, and when his brother breaks both his legs and moves back to California without his pain prescriptions, half the boarders are blissed out on OxyContin for an entire week. Luna's sister visits her evil stepmother and makes the trip worth her while by swiping some kind of crazy Mexican codeine that's illegal in the U.S.

But when the dorms run dry, desperate times call for desperate measures. On weekends when we're required to stay in the dorm, while I am locked in my room writing papers, the girls experiment with Salvia while the guys turn to Robo-tripping, which consists of chugging as much Robitussin as possible, throwing up, and then allegedly proceeding to "trip balls." One kid snorts muscle relaxants, which turn his snot orange and make his left tear duct leak uncontrollably. Although he insists he has a nice buzz, we don't join him.

"I think I'm going crazy," I tell Adam on the phone one Adderall-fueled evening. "I hate this. I've been memorizing these stupid, bullshit physics formulas all night, and even when I get the right answers, I still have no idea what they even *mean*."

"I know, babe, but you're so close! Try not to stress too much."

"Easy for you to say."

"I miss you."

"I miss you, too."

" . . . So, how's everything else going?"

"I told you! It's terrible! I'm not getting any sleep, and Cashmere totally shot me down in front of everybody in English, and I can't stand the—wait, are you typing?"

"What?"

"I can hear you typing!"

"No, no, I'm just—"

"Fine, whatever. You know what? I have to go anyway."

Click.

I finish my personal statement, perfect my résumé, and kiss the "Yale" on the address of my application envelope before dropping it off at the post office. That afternoon, I stroll into the lunch room for the first time in a long time to discover that my seat at the Great Eight table has been filled. I know I shouldn't be surprised, but I am. I think it's because college hysteria has led to Great Eight-like drama permeating every aspect of senior life. Even the toughest guys get teary-eyed after receiving low test grades, because everybody knows their futures are on the line. Every single grade counts. Diets become drastic. Caffeine might as well be injected by IV drip. I am complaining about the madness to Ms. Lynn when she asks me a question that will alter the entire course of my life.

"I'm actually writing a piece about teenage girls," she tells me. "The competitiveness, the pressure. I have the 'mother' and 'teacher' perspectives covered, but I was thinking it might be interesting to incorporate an opinion snippet from someone who's in the midst of it. Would you mind writing up a little candid diary entry about your experiences? I'd love to see it."

I am extremely flattered because I think the world of Ms. Lynn, so I readily agree. Later that night I rant about the backstabbing, the screaming fights that have erupted over who is asking which teachers for recommendations, the endless quest for skinniness. I lament about how, as compared to the fascinating collaborative discussions of CitySemester, classes here are all-out wars for conversational conquest— struggles to make the most insightful comment the soonest and most articulately, and to expose the weaknesses of the opposition if you suspect they aren't prepared. I forgo five hours of homework to write it. I let it all dribble out in one long rant, print a copy, and hand it in to Ms. Lynn the next day. She seems pleased. I, too, am pleased—until exactly twelve noon on December fifteenth, when my life is over.

My life is over. Not sarcastically or overdramatically. Just simply and completely over. I am deferred from Yale University, my dream school, my destiny. Did I mention my life is over? I'm a failure. Now it is official. I lie sprawled on the floor of Mrs. Berman's office until she pours a bottle of water over my face.

"Get up, love. Life does not end at seventeen."

"You have no idea what you're talking about! This was supposed to be my life!" I explain, shaking the Yale bluebook in her direction.

"When God closes one door, he—"

"Hangs up a noose," I interrupt.

For those who *did* get into their top colleges, the humble

way to express their dizzying relief would be to celebrate privately. The altruistic way would be to encourage those who are still embroiled in the yucky process. And then there's the bitchy way, the gloating way. The Sweatshirt Club is born.

The Sweatshirt Club is the Pearl Harbor of high school fashion, a devastating blow that threatens to break the resolve of even the staunchest social isolationists, prodding them toward unprecedented hostility and covetousness. It cuts across all previously established allegiances, pitting friends against friends and uniting total strangers in an elite fellowship whose membership is both irrefutable and inalterable. The golden ticket is an Early Action acceptance to your dream college and a concomitant desire to show it off.

Scanning the auditorium seats from the stage at each Morning Meeting, it is impossible not to spot the members—bold tops emblazoned with large block letters spelling out the stuff of dreams. COLUMBIA. CORNELL. Even though many of these human captions contain invisible subtext like PRINCETON (recruited athlete) or STANFORD (legacy), the constant reminder of my deferral is depressing, exhausting. A friend of mine who is rejected from Duke is forced to spend three classes a day seated across from a walking Duke billboard. Even those who didn't apply Early Action are haunted by the smug satisfaction with which these be-sweatshirted beacons of success glissade through classes, tests, and projects, safe in the knowledge that their asses are no longer on the line, that their transcripts are not subject to inspection with a fine-toothed comb, that their futures are secure.

My future sucks. Not only has my dream—the culmination of all of my studying and striving and volunteering—been crushed, but now I have only fifteen days to fill out fifteen more college applications. I try to imagine myself sunning in the quad at Pomona, skiing down the slopes of Middlebury, or hanging out in coffee shops near NYU, but nothing feels right. I've spent so much time imagining myself as a green Yale dot that everything else just seems wrong. Maybe I'll study journalism in Washington. Marine biology at the University of Hawaii? Maybe I'll go to pastry school. No, I'll be an international jewel smuggler! An international jewel smuggler with fifty-nine cats and a chocolate factory. I'll live on my own private island. Seriously, what the fuck am I doing with my life?

The very mention of "college" begins to send bursts of lava-hot hatred coursing through my veins. The Common Application was easy, but I feel like a psycho serial dater when I have to write fifteen different clichéd permutations of why I am absolutely in love with _____ University above all others, with its _____ courses, its _____ student body, and its unparalleled _____ _____. And the essays aren't the only lies. I look at my whole résumé with disdain. Not even my most outlandish embellishments can come close to matching the achievements Great Eighters warn about from competitors at rival schools. The faceless students snatching up our spots at the Ivies are world chess champions with professional photography exhibitions in New York City, National Merit Scholars who invented revolutionary energy-saving light bulb filaments and pushed the Harvard dean out of the way of a speeding bullet. It's madness.

As I slide one application after another into envelopes bound for California and Connecticut, I am struck by how thin they are. Is this really what four whole years of my life have amounted to—six pieces of printer paper? Sometimes I wonder if Dad might be right: if I should attach some amazing soundtrack to my application that would somehow elevate it beyond my GPA and SAT scores. It would shout, "Hey! I'm a real person! An interesting, passionate person who is going to make the most of everything your school has to offer. You won't regret it!" Clearly, nobody is ever going to get to know the real me by looking at my Common Application. But more and more, it seems like the real me is simply a lame generic version of the "studious private school class president," one of thousands upon thousands of others.

By the time I mail the last application, I actually begin to harbor a secret hope that I won't get in *anywhere* so I can justify packing my bags and moving to Mexico to become a lute-playing, peyote-growing shamanic minstrel or something. I long for the cheesy holistic-ness of CitySemester evaluations. I want to tell the admissions people all about my writing process, about the way World War II has figured into my creative unconscious via my grandmother's terrifying bedtime stories, about the fantastic jazz quartet I saw last weekend in Harlem whose tight, clean, seemingly simple ensemble work reminded me of the way Hemingway distills meaning with a few carefully chosen words. But they don't have time to care, and I can't waste more time thinking about it. I have to keep up my grades, run the student government, and withstand lunch table sneak attacks, all the while portraying a flawless example of leadership, poise, and beauty as I step onstage every morning in front of the entire school to make announcements. My reward for all of this was supposed to be a first-class pass to Yale, but ever since it was snatched away from me, a familiar little notion has begun to resurface, a recipe for perfection, that simple little question: *What would Scarlet do?*

chapter fifteen

DRUGS SUCK

My life is totally ruined, school bores me to tears, Adam and I are always bickering, and I've been gaining weight steadily since application season began. I just want to feel something different from the monotony of Danforth, so I do a little Erowid.com research. Cocaine sounds dangerous and sexy. Not wanting to seem like a total cokehead (in my misguided attempt to pattern my life after a total cokehead), I forego the usual channels of illicit retail (the stoners, the ravers, the kids who steal barbiturates from their parents' medicine cabinets) and begin to ask townies for tips. Turns out I needn't have looked any farther than the boys' dormitory. Julian has connections.

"You swear I won't, like, freak out?" I ask him as he arranges two white lines before me.

"Absolutely. It's nothing crazy. I mean, they used to put coke in kids' cough syrup."

I feel like one of those kids in the movies who are "up to no good" or "out on the lam" or "living on a prayer" or something as I stick a rolled-up hundred dollar bill in one nostril, hold the other closed, and inhale.

After ten seconds, light expands my forehead and pulses through my brain. I feel vast and bright. Who cares about all those stupid admissions officers and the Great Eight? I am brilliant and beautiful, and I can do whatever the fuck I want because I am fucking *great*.

Julian insists we go smoke a cigarette to "amp up the high." Just as we're about to go outside, we run into Dr. Putnam. *Shit*. I hope my heartbeat doesn't sound as loud as I think it does.

"Do you or do you not have academic detention today, Mr. Drake?"

Julian smiles a winning smile. "Well, you see, Dr. Putnam— and you're looking dashing today, I might add—I don't have any homework to do, and—"

"And?" Putz taps his foot with annoyance.

"Well, sir, I know academic detentions are intended for finishing homework, but I already *finished* all of my homework. So if you'll just excuse me—"

"I do not care, Mr. Drake, if you've just finished inventing a cure for cancer. You will sit in academic detention until it is through. And you, Miss Friedman, what on earth do you think you're wearing?" he balks, pointing in disgust to my pajama tank top. "What kind of example are you setting for the student body?"

Julian assumes a playfully grave expression. "Let me just say, Dr. Putnam, that I could not agree more. Just the *sight* of that tank top makes me want to commit grand theft auto."

After Julian goes into and then sneaks back out of detention, he leads me down past Rosewood through thickets of tangled brambles until the campus behind us disappears behind the trees. We emerge into a wide rectangular clearing overgrown with wild grass, like a long-abandoned tennis court, dotted with hundreds of purple flowers.

"Pretty, huh?" he asks.

"It's beautiful." I can't believe I've been at Danforth for four years and never found it.

"How did you find this place?"

"I'm kind of a wanderer," he says plainly.

We reach an enormous carpet of dead vines arching toward the sky. He separates a clump with his hand and motions for me to duck underneath. I step inside a massive overgrown tree whose many branches have curled down to form the walls of a perfect little wooden dome. It's tall enough for us to stand in, and even with the scattered beer bottles there's something a little bit magical about it—like the secret clubhouse I always wanted when I was a kid, a place where fairies might convene for evening meetings. Through the network of woven branches, the outside world seems pleasantly distant.

Julian lights a cigarette and motions grandly to the branches surrounding us. "So, you dig my digs?"

"I do—I do indeed dig."

"Yeah, I like it out here. Relaxing." He passes me a cigarette, and I take one because I want to be as relaxed as he looks. My first cigarette tastes horrible, like ashy mud, and I cough fitfully.

"Whoa there, pretty lady. First time?"

"Maybe."

"You get used to it. Don't inhale so much for now. And hey, let's see that winning cochair smile," he jokes. "Life is good."

I feel a calming buzz of disorientation pass behind my eyes

as I take my fourth puff. I sniff and feel a metallic sourness drip down the back of my throat, commingling with the smoke and sending pulses of pleasure radiating from my sinuses. Life is great, and I am a badass.

"Ahhh, you were right. This is nice."

"Told ya."

"Mmm." I close my eyes and imagine that there's nothing else outside the dome—no GPAs to return to, no more Putz ruining all of my best student government proposals, nothing but grass and leaves and sky.

"Whatcha thinkin' about?" Julian asks.

"I dunno." I take another drag. "Ever since the whole Yale thing, it's like the world is still moving but I'm hovering above it, just kind of . . . waiting. Like maybe there's something else, something bigger than all of this bullshit that I'm supposed to find—supposed to do."

"Like?"

I look at Julian. "If you had a choice between having a really fulfilling life, but everyone forgets who you were afterward, or a really meager life, and then after your death you somehow change the world in some remarkable way—like it turns out you end hunger or AIDS or something, but only after you're dead—which would you choose?"

"Happy now, anonymous later," he concludes definitively.

"But the other way legitimizes every single day. Wouldn't you want to know that all the toil and bullshit went toward something spectacu—"

"Well, sure, but I wouldn't know. 'Cuz I'd be dead."

"You mean maybe there's no path at all, and everything just . . . disappears?"

"Better live it up while you can," he tells me, his azure eyes twinkling.

I smile and repeat it, tasting the syllables, trying them on. "Better live it up while you can."

Adam and I are still dating long-distance, but phone relationships suck. He's always distracted, or I'm distracted, and there are long, awkward pauses and definitely no tickle fights. I start to dread his phone calls, but things are better when he returns for winter break. We go to a huge New Year's party in the City with the old hippie gang. Adam and I dance on a penthouse balcony overlooking a snowy Central Park and drink champagne.

I feel someone stroke my hair from behind. "I'm *everywhere*, Bana-nana." It's Ian. He sways.

"Are you okay, man?" Adam asks.

"He's fine," Trevor assures us, a cocktail glass in each hand. "Me and Luna tried that batch of acid last month. Good trips. He peaked a few hours ago."

"I am so *fine*," Ian giggles, studying the snow pattern on a wrought iron table. He looks up at us and assumes a playfully grave expression. "Just keep me away from the ledge." We laugh.

Inside, I notice Trevor sniffing a lot and disappearing into the bathroom every ten minutes or so, emerging like he's just been dipped in sunshine. I sidle up to him at the bar as he's pouring himself a Jack and Coke.

"You have blow?" I ask.

"Who's askin'?"

"I'm askin'."

He looks me up and down. "As a matter of fact, I do, Hannah Banana. You want a bump?"

I disappear with Trevor and emerge positively peachy. Everyone party-hops to a few more big bashes all around town—huge, seven-story private brownstone deals, packed from wall to wall with Prada and Pilsner Urquel. We go to a cavernous mansion on the Upper East Side that takes up an entire city block. There's even a private observatory on the roof. Trevor and I are doing a bump off the rim of a giant black Jacuzzi when Adam walks in on us.

"What the hell is this? Trevor, are you giving cocaine to my girlfriend? What the fuck is wrong with you, man?" I block Adam from lunging toward Trevor's neck.

"Hey! Trevor's not doing anything. It was my idea."

He stops. "Babe, what are you thinking?"

"It's not that intense. I mean, they used to put it in kids' cough syrup."

"Babe, that stuff can kill you."

Trevor shakes his head. "Naw, man, she's right. It's only dangerous if you blow, like, a whole table full. Plus," Trevor says, sitting on the rim of the Jacuzzi as he takes a joint out of his front pocket, "that shit's the finest in the City—none of the rat poison-cut crap you find in the 'burbs."

"I think you might like it, babe," I tell him.

He looks hesitant. "I don't know . . . "

"Well, don't try it if you have your doubts, but—I don't know, I really like it."

Trevor sparks up the J and slides smoothly backward into the empty Jacuzzi. "Plus, it makes sex insaaane," he laughs.

Adam checks the door to make sure it's locked. "All right,

I'm trying it." Trevor passes him the dollar bill. "Who would have thought *you'd* become a bad influence on *me?*" he says, playfully patting me on the butt. He leans down. "So I just . . . "

"Yep," says Trevor.

Adam sniffs in, his eyes grow wide, and he squinches up his nose.

"What do you think?"

He rolls his neck around. "Hmm . . . I don't know, baby. I prefer the ganga, but I guess it's fun in, like, an upper sort of way."

"See?"

"You're always right," he smiles, then makes a face. "Tastes like ass, though." We hear everyone in the ballroom counting down to midnight, and I lead him away from Trevor onto the terrace just in time for the ball to drop at midnight. We share a perfectly amazing passionate New Year's Eve kiss. But soon enough winter break ends, and I return to hell—I mean, school.

I'm smoking a cigarette with Julian in the forest when I get a call from *Newsweek*.

"Shut the fuck up. Who is this?"

"Excuse me, is this Hannah Friedman?" The woman's tone is confident and professional, and there's no giggling in the background.

"Um—sorry, who is this again?"

"This is Regina Linzer from *Newsweek* magazine. I received your article about the college application process from a colleague, and I'd like to publish it in our *My Turn* section."

Ohmigod.

"Is this Hannah Friedman, or should I try an alternate numb—?"

"No, this is her—I mean, me. I—sorry, I thought you were someone else. But, yes! I mean, wow, whatever you need. You really want to publish it?"

"Absolutely. It'll come out in the April issue, just in time for admissions decisions. Timely content that captures a unique voice."

Ecstatic, I call Adam that evening. "They're publishing me in *Newsweek*!"

"That's so great, babe."

"You don't sound excited."

"I am. That's great, babe."

"Aren't you surprised?"

"Not really," he says absently.

"I didn't even know they submitted it! I almost fell on the floor when I got the phone call, why aren't you surpri—"

"I'm just not, okay? Don't give me a hard time for having faith in you. Jeez."

"Sorry."

Silence.

I lie back in bed and stare at the ceiling. "Listen, I should go. I have work to do."

"Okay."

"Talk to you soon."

"Bye."

Click.

Julian and I swipe an electronic scale from the physics department to make sure we're not getting ripped off by his drug dealer. I find that coke makes class discussions surprisingly enjoyable. Another line. Another multiple-choice test. Another morning of standing up in front of the entire school pretending that I am perfect. I soar with every inhale, above homework and student government and deferrals, but after a few weeks the crash is devastating. Aggravation scrapes at me. The light that once expanded my head has bored a funnel into the very center of my brain, through which noxious tar surges. Drip, drip, drips. Sears.

Another line. Everything is fine.

I'm disappointed that I haven't become the frail, ravishing vision of Scarlet by now. I thought the coke would suppress my appetite, but instead, when I'm high I just eat faster. *Perfect.* I run three miles and then smoke a half a pack of cigarettes. I wake up lamenting last night's dinner and go to bed planning tomorrow's breakfast. I scowl at my flabby chubby cheeks in every bathroom mirror and do a bump off the sink before returning to class, where I quote dead white historians and philosophers and authors in exchange for hearty praise and good grades. Well done, well done. Gold stars all around.

One wonderful Friday, the boredom temporarily subsides. I feel like a literary goddess as a *Newsweek* photo shoot crew follows me all around campus like paparazzi. Julian invites me to his house that weekend to celebrate my success.

He smiles mischievously, and his azure eyes twinkle as he holds up the tiny square of paper.

"So, you definitely can't, like, go insane?" I ask him, still a little nervous.

"Nah. I mean, maybe if you drink like a *shot glass* full. But the guys in the dorm all tried two tabs from this batch last weekend. Take a half. It'll be mild."

I put the pinkie nail-sized paper on my tongue. We turn off the lights and prepare by putting on Pink Floyd and turning on the iTunes visualizer. I lie down next to Julian on top of his little-boy baseball sheets in his seaside mansion, and we listen and wait.

"Do you feel anything?"

"No. Do you?"

"No."

We wait and listen. I start to wonder if the darkness seems any different, thicker, more velvety, or if I'm just sleepy, but mostly I concentrate on Julian reaching out and touching my hand with his. I know I should pull away but I don't. His hand is warm, strong, safe. The music is—trumpets are triumphant. It is dark now because the day is gone. Sometimes everything ends. Always. I peer past the lovely velvet—

VvvAM! The crust of the universe cracks, expelling an explosive flare of solarized pink satin—a thousand fingers condemning in every dimension—and I am standing, and I am falling, and I am out. Alone in the hallway, and the drunken carpet snaps into frame for a flash. A noise. It's like metal spoons and blood. Julian's mother's voice envelops me, and I run.

I run down hallways, millions of hallways, and through paintings and passages, past the melting windows until >>><!!><>>? an alligator devours my arm. Mom? The sharp pain snaps me into a second of sobriety and I realize I have run straight into a large decorative cactus. Julian's mother's pink satin pajamas. She must have walked in. And now my arm is a decorative cactus. But clarity is like ice cream and mirror-me devours it and now I know, I KNOW, that this is how I'm going to die. It's all been leading up to this for years—the books and the tests and the boys and the lies and now . . .

I pull the tiny, sharp missiles out of my arm, and the blood tastes green. Time is gone. Julian is gone. I am gone. I cry beneath the cactus for forty-seven earth years.

Panic. Nazis. It is not safe here. They could find me in the morning. I need to get back to the guest room. As long as I get back to the guest room, my (cactus) world (where?) will not (never) fall into total photal disarray.

Azure eyes. I am in the guest room. I grab my notebook like an anchor to reality because maybe it will keep me from going insane if I can just—I cannot. I cannot just. I cannot *anything* because everyone is watching me.

Julian's guest room is filled with portraits of old, dead relatives, and they stare with more than disapproval. Surely they are going to eat my soul. Eyes yes eyes eyes i yeseyeseyeseyes. I pull the covers over my head and tremble and wish and wish that my brain weren't broken. I turn off the lights to make the eyes go away, but then they cut loose from portrait-moorings and hover over the covers.

Julian finally finds me after the eyes are illuminated by daylight.

"You okay?" His pupils are huge and he is pale and manic and mischievous and I do not trust him.

I want to yell at him for this, for abandoning me, but all I get out is, "You found me."

"Of course I found you. You were—"

"I was lost," I insist quickly. I have more to say, but no possible way to say it. "I'm lost."

"You need a cigarette."

"No! I—"

"C'mon, you can still see the moon through the trees."

Determined not to be left alone, I follow him outside. He massages my neck on the sloping cartoon terrace underneath the truffala trees. I can think now, but it's all in this hazy bubble. We go back inside and he gets me a bowl of cereal. He drops me off at the train station. I go through the motions of buying a ticket and sitting on the train, but I know I am not normal. Something is wrong, like an invisible cloud of confusion is following me, like I am underwater.

On my way out of the train station to meet my mother I am thrown backward onto the sidewalk by a stranger. I gasp and realize I have so narrowly avoided being hit by a bus that a crowd has frozen around me, anticipating the disaster. They sigh with relief and trickle off.

"What the hell were you thinking?"

" . . . I wasn't."

I get in Mom's car wearing my sunglasses and pretend to be exhausted so that I can avoid her usual barrage of questions. I can piece together reality now, but I still feel like it's behind thick, foggy glass, like my head is submerged in a fish tank of clear Jell-O. Something is really not right, and I hope she can't tell. I hope I'm not going to be stuck like this forever. *What if I never—*

"Did you have a good time?" she asks.

"Mmm hmm."

"Was Dot as nutty as ever?"

She thinks I went to Cashmere's. I run with it. "Yup."

We pull into the driveway. She locks the car doors. "Would you like to tell me what you're doing with this?" Mom pulls the electronic scale out of her purse.

I'm way too out of it to risk spinning some elaborate yarn about take-home physics assignments. I can barely even get out two words. Mom stares at me disappointedly as I scramble through the fog to explain, and I feel my lips murmur, "It's Julian's."

"Who?"

"This—he's this kid from school. I'm holding it for him."

Mom eyes me warily. I don't think she bought it. "Are you *hung over?*"

"No!"

"I knew those bratty princesses weren't as prim and proper as they seemed."

I sleep for eighteen hours straight and wake up feeling a little less submerged, a little more in control. A few days later, I flip to a fresh page of my journal and find a curious but halfway-familiar scrawl on the opposite page, scribbly hieroglyphs from the past.

What if everything
EVERYTHING
is leading up to
THIS MOment?

chapter sixteen

EVERYTHING SUCKS

I am writing my billionth thesis paper. Or maybe it's a billion and one. Either way, it is yet another brain-numbingly dumb exercise in telling my teacher what I know he wants to hear, with five sentences of analysis flanked by ten pages of big, fancy words. He loves it every time. Just a matter of cranking it out. Again. I watch the cursor blink against another blank page, and I feel a sudden compulsion to eat macaroni and cheese. It'll be a nice break: leave my room, heat it up in the microwave, sit at the table and read *Vogue*, take my mind off things. I deserve this macaroni and cheese. It turns out I also deserve half a meatball sub and a Snickers before I sneak into the dorm store and steal gummy worms and marshmallow Peeps by the mouthful. By the time I return to the blank page, my stomach is enormous. The stacks of books, the huge pile of dirty laundry—I wish I could crumple myself into the hamper like a pair of muddy jeans and just disappear until high school is over.

When I'm feeling particularly disgusting, I usually chew a

few squares of chocolate laxatives and wait for everything to come out so I can feel clean again, pure. I eat half the pack and stuff the rest back in my drawer. My fingers brush against a long-lost Adderall. I try to crush it between the folded halves of a piece of computer paper with a book, but it's not strong enough, so I balance the pill underneath the leg of my desk chair and sit. When it's pulverized into powdery blue dust, I snort it through a milkshake straw before picking up *Wuthering Heights* again.

Now I page through it manically and without the usual hesitation. Themes, plot arcs, I am ruthless as I tear apart the symbolism, like a monster, like I'm taking no goddamn *Wuthering* prisoners. Quote. Intro. Thesis. I squeeze it all out from my lazy insides with uncommon focus, with revulsion. Right around the fifth page I start getting cramps. My stomach is knotted with raw, fiery ropes, and I have to lie down to keep from crying out loud. The pain is hot and all-consuming, and I live inside it for a while, curling my knees up to my chin.

I feel the fiery knots traveling lower and lower until I know it's time to release them. Finally. I feel clean for the first time in hours. But it only lasts for as long as it takes to wash my hands, by which time I realize I'll have to return to the paper again. I punch my thigh. I wake myself up with a slap in the face. *Look what you did,* I hear as I watch the mirror. *Look at you, you fat, lazy piece of shit. You did it again. Happy now?* I stare in revulsion at my stomach pooch, wash my face, and march back to the blinking cursor.

Thesis, transition, topic sentence . . . footnotes. Endless footnotes. I'm formatting footnotes when Luna's sister dashes into my room clad only in a Mexican blanket and collapses onto my bed. Usually she's having a fight with her mother, or her father is a fascist, or the art department doesn't think that decapitated doll heads qualify as a legitimate artistic medium, but tonight she is quiet and doesn't start ranting so I feel like something is really wrong. Her face is puffy and red.

"Ian's dead," she says quietly.

Breath is sucked out of me. My body is hurled into orbit at a million miles an hour as my brain struggles to form words with no oxygen. Maybe she's kidding. "Are you serious?"

"He's dead."

The boys' dorm finds out via text message, and suddenly there is a flurry of IMs back and forth, confirming and contradicting information. He was found in his dormitory. His roommate found him. It was a seizure. An overdose. No, a fluke accident.

I am nauseous. This is real. This is crisis, and panic, and I feel hot and angry. I am sick. I am trapped in my dorm room and trapped in high school with friends who don't know and teachers who don't care—and he's Dead? Like that? People just die like that? We cry. Pace. I find a picture of Amelia picking through Ian's hair at my kitchen table, from the party Adam and I threw over Christmas break. Everything is falling apart.

Focus. At 3:24 AM I finish the paper, but my legs are twitching. My torso buckles, too, in jarring rhythm. I get into bed and watch the glaring green alarm clock in the empty darkness. Laundry, guitar, Ian's curls, YaleYaleYale, Ian's fingerprints—they swirl all around, slicing my mind like thin little razors, severing sanity. I try to piece everything back together into one coherent lump, but I'm all alone and the voice is deafening. *That was an idiotic quote you made yesterday onstage. Those whispers were about you. Everyone in your English class hates you. Your stomach makes me want to vomit. Vomit. You have no friends. You're a pathetic excuse for a musician, and you'll never get any better. You are and always will be fatfatfatfatfatfatFAT.* I punch myself in the arm and get out of bed, magnetically drawn to the zippered compartment in the back of my wallet where I keep the razor Julian gave me for cutting coke. Unzip. Razor. Sliiice. I'm quiet.

Just for this sliver of a moment, then once, twice, three more slivers. For three more moments I am quiet as I slice. And I bleed. Gliding the razor across my skin with measured, painterly strokes, the pigment seeps out red red red. Blood beads to rivulets and pretty little berry droplets drip. The saltiest sap.

I carve a lattice into my arm, thin and deep. But I do not want to kill myself. I do not want to kill myself. I don't deserve to die—I'm too disgusting. But maybe . . .

Maybe I can change. Even though it's never worked before, maybe this is the big, momentous wake-up call. Finally. Maybe this time I'll stay on the diet, I'll practice guitar every day, I'll have a hundred friends, I'll get into Yale and get rich and buy my parents a new house and win an Oscar and lose twenty-five pounds and marry a prince and—

Slice, *slice*. This time as punishment. Reality check. *Who do you think you are, ugly girl? Who the fuck do you think you are?* A fraud. Nobody sees what a fraud I am. How often I pretend. Everything about me is not good enough, and it's all my fucking fault. I cut deeper. I can't breathe. My hand shakes so hard that the razor clatters to the floor. I leave it there and

taste the blood and shake and shake and try to breathe and—
ah . . . ah . . . ah . . .

I mean to call Adam. I want to call Adam. I am going to call
Adam.

But this is not a fairy tale.

"What's going on? What's wrong?" Julian is immediately
concerned by my unexpected late night phone call, worry that
is magnified when all he hears is silence on the other end. I
can barely talk.

"I—I tried to, I had this . . . and Ian, I—"

"Are you okay?"

"I'm, I just—fuck. It's an ah, ah—"

"I'm coming over."

"No!"

"I'm coming over."

I prop open the third-floor door and sneak down to let him
in. He gathers me up in a firm hug, the kind of hug you get in
movies when you're reunited with your family after an earth-
quake rips through half of California or you just survived the
sinking of the *Titanic*. Everything is spinning. Life is suspended in a milky mist. I rest my head on Julian's shoulder
and he strokes my hair. I am all out of tears, so I stare at the
ceiling and count tiles. *Fuck college. Fuck everyone.* What the
hell is even the point if you could be nonexistent tomorrow?

"I don't want to die like this," I say, finally.

"Like what?"

"Like this—cramming for tests and worrying about whether
or not the footnotes are—"

"I love you, you know."

He kisses me.

I am blank. All out of tears, all out of energy. I live in the kiss for as long as it lasts. Of course I've thought about this before, but I never thought we would actually—but Adam . . .

"I can't," I tell him.

Julian nods. "I know. I just thought you should know." He holds me.

I wake up alone.

Two days later, my cell phone rings. It's Adam. He's crying. "Sorry, I didn't mean to wake you."

"What's wrong? Are you okay?"

" . . . I got arrested."

"What?! What do you mean? What happened?"

"What am I gonna tell my parents, Hannah?"

"Honey, what happened?"

"We were hanging out in this girl's room, smokin' weed, a little booze, a little coke, nothing too crazy, and then the campus police knocked on the door. Her friends bolted out the window, but I figured it wouldn't be right to just leave her there to take the rap for everybody's stash, so I said it was mine."

"You took the fall for other people's drugs?"

"Everyone's always talking about how lax the campus police are here. I figured it'd be a few hours of community service or something, *max*, but they saw the coke and they, they—"

I've never heard Adam whimper before.

"My parents are gonna disown me. What the fuck am I gonna do?"

"We'll get it all sorted out. You—"

"Ah, shit, *shit*. Babe, I gotta go."

"Wait, wait! Where are you goi—"

"I love you." He hangs up the phone.

Putz has the nerve to show up at Ian's funeral. There's a line outside the viewing room, and we whisper disgustedly when we see him arrive. We sit and shuffle our feet, and after half an hour of standing in line, we almost forget we're waiting to see a dead person. I eat an entire half-loaf of complimentary pound cake in anticipation. When we finally file into the main room, I see the blonde curls coming out of the coffin and I flip. I can't breathe. I will my feet to take me forward. Ian. He looks plastic—overly groomed and dressed in a three-piece suit. I'm pretty sure they put blush on him because he's usually much paler. But it's still him. Ian. Hippied-out, sandal-wearing, pot-smoking, dead Ian in a three-piece suit. I wonder if he would think this was funny.

He looks so real that I expect him to tell us he's only joking. I have to silence the urge to reach out and touch his face just to make sure. Next to the casket is a poster of pictures of him, helping out at soup kitchens and laughing with friends. I wonder if, under the curl of some quantum time lapse, he is still at all of those places, lively and alive. Or maybe he's here in spirit, or in our hearts.

I realize it's all crap. He's gone. He's dead, and he couldn't be more dead. I want someone to say something peaceful and melodic about how people live on in our memories, how no one is alone, but I force myself to stare at his dead body and face the fact that there is no happy message, no sing-song consolation that can explain away the fact that no matter what he used to be, now he's just a big slab of Gone.

I wish there was something to say good-bye to. But the hair, the rosy cheeks, the three-piece suit—it's like everything has been sucked out of him, and his body stuffed full of preservatives like a sleeping-bag shell. It's sick. I'm sick. The line trudges onward to where his parents and brother are piously shaking hands with the visitors. Trevor is ahead of me. Ian's mother takes his hand.

"I'm sure you could tell me some good stories about my son," she says. "I think now, now that I can't worry anymore, we'll laugh about them someday."

Trevor is stunned, and I think he is speechless for the first time ever. Embarrassed. "Yes, ma'am," he nods. Then he looks to the side and runs his hand through his scruffy chestnut beard. His lip quivers, and Ian's mother pulls him close to her in one swift motion. He's crying.

"Ian loved you boys," she says to Trevor and the gang. "Thank you for being such good friends." They shuffle past and hang their heads. Ian's father reaches out to shake my hand. I can't believe that, after everything they've gone through, this family is standing around comforting *us*. I think they are the bravest family in the whole world. They are compassionate and graceful and strong, and they don't deserve this.

We stand outside and smoke. I thought I might not want to at a funeral. I should be cherishing life or something, but this is ceremonial—things suck so badly that cigarettes are simply required. We don't talk. We just smoke. Julian's mother picks us up to take us back to school. She drops us off, but it's before curfew and we feel weird. How could dorm rules possibly apply after we just saw our dead friend zipped up in a three-piece suit? We don't give a fuck. We walk down to the river. Up again. Past the abandoned church. We smoke.

By the time we arrive back on campus it's well past lights-out, and we stop where the road splits, heading down the hill to the girls' dorms and up to the boys'. We stand there at the fork for a while. I can see through my dorm room window from here. Dirty laundry. Silently, I take Julian's hand.

"Where to, kid?" he asks.

Together, we walk slowly up the road.

Adam decides he can't face his family, so he gets an apartment near campus. Every time I talk to him, things seem more and more dire. It's unbelievably depressing.

"I got a free couch off the side of the street today," he says, trying to sound upbeat.

"Adam, come home. This is ridiculous."

"You know I can't do that."

"What the hell are you doing out there? You're going to work in fast food for the rest of your life, sleeping on couches you found in the garbage?"

"It was on the *street,* not in the garbage."

"Whatever! You need to come home and get your fucking act together. Your parents are worried about you. I'm worried about you!"

"I can't."

"Adam, I—"

"Hannah, I *can't.* I just need a few more months to get back on my feet. My whole life, people have been picking up my messes, and my parents just . . . I can't do that to them again. I need to do this on my own."

"I think you're wrong. I think you're just scared to—"

"Listen, I gotta go," he says quietly.

"Fine."

"Love you."

I hang up the phone.

Mrs. Berman is hugging me tightly to her bosom. I'm not really sure why, but I'm having a crappy day and her bosom is very soft, so I just kind of go with it.

"Come with me!" she announces, grabbing my hand. She leads me into her office and around the back of the desk, clasping her hands beneath her chin. "Type in your name."

"Why?"

"Just enter it."

Hmm. I type in my name and press ENTER.

Suddenly, marching band music comes pouring out of the speakers and a big picture of a bulldog pops up onto the screen. A Yale bulldog. It takes me a second to realize what's going on.

"I got *in*?!"

"Didn't I tell you I look out for my babies?"

"I GOT IN?!"

Never has a single moment been so completely, utterly gratifying. Maybe it *does* pay to drive yourself crazy staying up nights writing papers. I am a GREEN Yale dot. Yale is my destiny. Wait—if Yale knew they wanted me, couldn't they have let me in way back in December and saved me all these months of agony instead of deferring me and making me wriggle around like a worm on a hook? What was the point? I wonder about it for a few brief moments before I am overtaken with joy again. Everything is perfect. I'm going to Yale.

Eventually Adam comes home, but all of his friends are still at college, and he's different. Despondent. Woeful and obnoxious. Every time I see him I feel awful. Guilty. He can't smoke pot because he has to undergo regular drug testing, all of his new poetry is dark and depressing, and I'm getting ready to go to Yale while he flounders about with no plan whatsoever. I can't take it anymore.

"Mom, what am I supposed to do?" I lament, sprawling myself across the kitchen table. "I'm the one who told him to come back to New York, and now I just . . . I'm not having fun anymore. He seems so lost."

"I think you need to either commit to fixing things or break it off and stop leading him on."

I don't like this idea. I want to keep all the nice parts of Adam and erase all the annoying ones. I want him to be at my beck and call, but I don't want to feel tied down. I know it's irrational. Selfish.

"Plus, you're going to college soon," Mom reminds me. "Long-distance relationships take an awful lot of work. And don't you want to have your options open when you get to Yale?"

She's right.

"I think we have to break up," I tell him over the phone that night. I've turned the decision over and over in my head, weighing the pros and cons. I planned the words carefully, but the minute they escape from my mouth, I start to wish I could reach out and take them back.

"But I came back to New York . . . for you."

"I know. But . . . " *What am I doing? What about the poetry? His warm chest and the— No. He's holding me back. But—* "I just think, you know, with me going off to college and everything . . . I still lo—"

"Good-bye, Hannah."

Click.

I remember the darkroom and Mormon Christmas and marshmallows and condoms and kisses, and I start to cry a little. I never meant to break that poor boy's heart.

Ever since the night of Ian's death I swore I'd never touch cocaine again, and I swore I'd never kiss Julian again. Although I don't like to admit it, I've done a little of both here, a little of both there, and since breaking up with Adam, more and more everywhere. Julian is gorgeous. I'm bored of school, of life. I'm a Yalie now, but nothing will really change until I get to New Haven. More papers, more mindless memorization, more cookies, more coke. By spring, I am completely out of cash.

Next to the zippered compartment in my wallet where I keep my razor is a lone credit card that Dad gave me to use in the event of an emergency. I'm talking apocalyptic, kidnapped, zombie-epidemic emergency. But I think he might not notice if I take out just a little bit of money, seeing as he manages money the same way one might manage a herd of octopi—which is to say, not very efficiently. As I walk to the Stop & Shop ATM, my mind is clouded with all the reasons this is a terrible idea.

Don't do it.

Why not? He barely notices anything!

But it's wrong . . . and he trusts you.

But it's just this once!

By the time I enter the PIN code, there's no looking back. Crisp twenties flow out of the machine like magic right into my hand. I feel guilty only for as long as it takes to get the money to the dealer, and as soon as we make the trade, my mind is onto other things. Greedy, needy cravings that have gone unheeded for too many days.

I never thought I'd be one of those slippery-slope type of girls, but here I am, naked and wasted and puking up brown Jägermeister juice, waiting for the last acrid drop to come out so I can wipe off my nose and do another line. There's nothing but the line. This one and the next one, which Julian has cut out on my bedside table. I devour the bigger one.

"Hey, that was mine."

"Not anymore."

He reaches to brush against my thigh.

"Get the fuck away from me," I spit, pushing him back across the bed.

It hasn't been a good night. I feel an ocean of distance between me and the whole world. I want to disappear into the nucleus of my balled-up pillow and just never come out again. We are bickering. I want him to take things more seriously. He's too possessive. I'm tired of him calling me at 2 AM on weekends when he's drunk, walking down the side of the highway in the rain because he's had another fight with his parents. He thinks everything is a joke. He's the life of the entire party, until he's the most stubborn asshole I've ever met. The coke craving sucks. It's a pounding searing emptiness that penetrates, pins you to the bed. Heart races. I try not to move or breathe too heavily because it sends waves of bile lapping up toward my throat.

"Ugh." I throw up in the garbage can again.

We fuck. The sweaty rhythm keeps me sane as I ride him. I take a swig of Jägermeister and feel a brief soaring high as the liquid goes deeper down my throat, but soon I can slowly feel myself coming down again: farther, faster, darker. My heart is pounding and my throat is raw and sore. Cigarette— that should do the trick. I just want to feel good.

Tonight I crash harder than ever before. I puke all over my carpet and lie in bed, my eyes pinned open, staring at the ceiling, trying not to touch any part of Julian as I squeeze into the corner of the bed, praying for sleep, for relief from this electrified gloom—an active gloom that burrows and screeches and tears at you from within. More coke. Settle things down.

Now that all the seniors have gotten into college, we're just biding our time at Danforth. Classes are a joke. Tests are a joke. Senioritis overtakes us. All the hours we pretended to care about bullshit reading responses and after-school activities are now filled with a lot of drunken, lazy revelry. Nobody gives a fuck, and the teachers can't do anything about it. The only card administration still holds is the fact that our admission can be rescinded if we screw up really badly. It's just enough pressure to keep us coming to class, but not enough to make us actually try. We coast. We do the absolute least amount of work possible to maintain a passing average, and we wait. For freedom. For real life. Whatever that means.

On April nineteenth my article is published in *Newsweek*.

It's amazing to see my name in print, though when Ms. Lynn asked me to write a diary entry all those months ago, I never intended to share my social and academic qualms with the entire nation. The *Newsweek* editor explained we would have to cut out anything that didn't directly relate to college in order to fit the word count. After all the editing, what's left is a scathing indictment of the Danforth college application process.

I'm not in love with the picture they chose. It's a staunch "studently" pose of me holding a bunch of carefully stacked books outside Putz's office. But nobody would be able to tell it's Danforth. It's just a generic, stately stone building. I don't mention the name of the school or any of the students, though many anonymous Great Eighters populate the anecdotes throughout the piece. Hopefully people will appreciate my candid account of the horrors of the college application process.

Mom and I take the day off to celebrate my debut as a professional author. We give Amelia a bath and then go to a movie, stopping to feed the ducks down by the train station.

When I come back to school on Friday, it's like I'm in one of those movies where someone died but doesn't know they're dead yet. People look right through me. All whispers and giggles are silenced when I walk by as if I'm accompanied by an eerie cold front. A bold girl in the year below me whose father owns half of Manhattan is the first one to congratulate me.

"Lying to get published? Real classy, bitch."

Wowza. During the day, things only get worse. Great Eighters treat me like I have the plague. I get shoved from behind in the hallway and turn around to find nobody there. A copy of the article is pinned to the bulletin board, my eyes gouged out with pins. Whispers follow me. I am in one big paranoid "everyone-is-talking-about-me" nightmare. But this time, everyone really *is* talking about me. Mrs. Berman finds me in the hall.

"Glad to see you're still intact."

"What do you mean?"

She holds up a copy of my article.

"Like it?" I ask her.

"You caused quite a stir in the faculty lounge this morning."

"Really?"

"Are you kidding? My voice is hoarse from defending your honor. You have to be careful who you implicate in national news publications, Hannah. Administration is not amused."

"I didn't implicate anybody. The school is anonymous."

"Administration doesn't think so."

"It's an opinion piece! Everyone knows the college application process is tota—"

"Listen to me when I tell you to tread lightly, my love. Let's just get through this year. And tread lightly."

Later on, someone taps my shoulder impatiently in the hallway, and I'm in the process of swinging around to slap their hand away when I realize it's Mac.

"Pretty big stuff, Lois Lane," he says, blocking my swat. "Gotta work on those reflexes though."

"What'd you think?"

"I'm proud of you."

"Thanks."

He gives me a hug. "Seriously, you impress me. But if anyone asks, I think you're the she-Judas. Can't let the masses know I'm consorting with the 'frenemy.'"

I laugh and give him a shove. "You really kicked ass in Executive Committee yester—"

Putz appears from out of nowhere. "A word, Miss Friedman?"

I follow him into his office, turning over my shoulder to stick out my tongue at Mac.

Putz has me sit in a tiny folding chair facing his desk. He paces around me with wide strides. "Well, well, well, Miss Friedman." He stops. "We have been made aware of your . . . document."

"My *document?*"

"Document."

"The article?"

He glares at me steely-eyed above his glasses. He nods. "And we would like to *strongly* suggest that you write a retraction," he says curtly.

"What?"

"And if you were compensated for this . . . document, I think it would behoove you to return the funds immediately."

"Are you *serious?*"

Putz sneers. "Always."

"Um, with all due respect, Dr. Putnam, I stand by what I wrote."

"I thought you might," he replies, strolling over to his armchair. "If you *do* decide to write a retraction, the board members and I will be eager to read it. If not," he lowers himself down onto the leather cushion and joins his hands together, "then I hope you will be fully prepared to face your critics."

I nod politely, thank him for his time, and get the heck out of there as quickly as possible.

Mac greets me in the hallway. I am still shell-shocked. He must be able to tell.

"Someone looks spooked. Was Putnam hiding the KGB in his candy dish?"

"They want me to re*tract* the article and send back the money!"

"Tough break."

I slide down onto the bench outside the office, incredulous. "Can you be*lieve* that shit?"

"You can't?"

"Where are we, *Oceania*? Who are they, the Ministry of *Truth*? They're gonna nail me for some *thought crime* against the—"

"Spare me the Orwellian déjà vu, Friedman. All I'm—"

"Don't call me Friedman."

"Fine, *your authorliness*," he pronounces with a grand bow. "All I'm saying is, I'm proud of you for speaking your mind, but you can't expect me to believe you had no idea you'd be stepping on some toes here."

"What do you mean? I didn't use any names!"

"You didn't name the people you insulted in an internationally circulated periodical, so you thought they'd be, what, lining the halls to throw you a ticker-tape parade?"

"Well, I don't know. I hadn't really thought about it."

He puts his hands into his huge green jacket and falls back

onto the bench, somewhat less gracefully than planned. "Remember that play in the old train station your mom took us to see last November?"

"Mmm-hmm."

"We snuck out and sat in the pavilion on the river, and you told me you used to talk to the man in the moon, and then I told you that you must have been an extremely gullible child."

"I remember. Why are we talking about this?"

"Because then you asked me if I'd ever want to go up there. To the moon. And I said, 'Of course, wouldn't you?' And you said no, because it would be unaffordable. And that even if it were affordable, they'd skimp on safety precautions for publicity's sake, just like with the *Challenger*. And that having your period in space would probably be like being haunted by the interdimensional ectoplasm from *Poltergeist*."

"Eiw, did I really say all that?"

"You really did. My point being, if you worried about spaceship disasters in the hypothetical future, you must have envisioned this scenario once or twice before sending the thing in. That's all I'm saying."

Hmm.

"If you ask me, you got what you asked for."

I bite my lip. I hate it when he's right.

Feeling guilty, that night I get out the school contact list and dial up every one of the girls in my English class. Cashmere, Teagan, the Bs, everybody. I try to explain that the article began as more of a diary entry, that I hadn't intended to hurt anybody. Some of them are gracious, and others are clearly pissed off. Cashmere seems particularly miffed. "I hope you're pleased with yourself," she tells me. I try not to think about it too much. *Just get to the end of the year and you're out of here.*

Putz stares down at Julian and me, chewing his fat lower lip as the corners of his mouth turn upwards in taut satisfaction. I count the purply veins on his head as he taps his fingers on the arm of his leather chair. Tap-a-tap-tap. Tap-a-tap-tap.

Finally he speaks. "The game is up."

Julian and I look at each other, completely perplexed. *Did he hear us curse in the hallway or something?*

"There are witnesses," Putz declares ominously. Then he explains that we have been accused, by several anonymous sources, of committing "unmentionably lascivious acts" in the private library of Rosewood Palace.

Julian bursts out laughing. "You think . . . wait, wait, you think we busted in there, snuck up the stairs, and had *sex* in the—"

"This is hardly a laughing matter, Mr. Drake," Putz hisses. "Do you have anything to say for yourselves?"

"Are you *serious*?" Julian squeals in a falsetto fit of giggles.

"Dr. Putnam, we have no idea what you're talking about," I explain with composure, elbowing Julian because his laughter is obviously not helping matters at all.

"There's really no need to go through the motions of denial," Putz explains coolly. "We have witnesses. And in addition to being unspeakably disrespectful, this is a serious health issue, which is why I've invited your parents here to discuss the consequences."

Julian goes white.

236

Putz leads us death-march style into the adjoining office. Our parents sit in a semicircle of pinstriped armchairs looking very confused.

"What the hell is this?" Mom asks me as the door closes. "Do you have AIDS?"

Putz explains the twisted allegations to our parents, emphasizing how *deeply* disappointed he is in our disrespectful conduct, and how *deeply* dismayed he is to have to report the offense to our future colleges. We're being suspended. He expresses his *deepest* sympathies at the possibility that our colleges will choose to rescind our acceptance based on this very serious disciplinary matter, and explains that he'll be happy to collaborate with our parents on further disciplinary action, given the seriousness of the circumstances. When he's finished, he folds his hands and assumes a look of earnest concern. "Thank you for your time," he says. "I only regret we had to meet under such . . . unfortunate circumstances."

My mom shakes her head. "Pffft, ex*cuse* me? Are you planning on telling me what you're accusing my daughter of before you suspend her?"

Putz seems slightly unsettled. "I don't think it would be appropriate to discuss the *exact* details," he replies quickly, "but I can assure you—"

"I can assure *you* that if you call me out of work for a health emergency concerning my daughter, and then make me wait two hours without telling me anything while I wonder what kind of horrible *disease* she's contracted, then you'd better have some details," Mom snaps.

The outburst catches Putz off guard. This is clearly not how the scene played out in his head. "There are witnesses," he repeats soberly. "If you'll excuse me, I have to attend to something for a moment. I'll leave you to discuss Hannah and Julian's . . . indiscretion."

Mom's eyes widen. "What did he say your name was?"

"Julian."

My mother folds her arms. "Would you like to tell me why my daughter was hiding your electric drug scale in her room?"

Uh-oh.

Julian looks at her like she's nuts and says he has no idea what she's talking about.

I feel my face flush. "Mom, can we talk about this later?"

She stands up. She's the ringleader now, and she loves having the floor. She struts across the office with an air of satisfaction. "Oh no, we're going to talk about this *now*."

"Are you accusing my son of dealing drugs?" Julian's mother asks, appalled.

"Where did it come from, Hannah?" Mom asks sharply.

She's baiting me like a bear. I want to claw her eyes out. "Mom . . . *please*."

"Where did it come from?"

I pray for everything to pause. I know my mother is enjoying the fact that I cannot escape to my room and slam the door. I need time to think. To cover my tracks. As the silence swells and the room closes in all around me, I glance over at Julian and beg him with my eyes to say something, anything. To rescue me. He meets my gaze, then looks to my mother.

"It's not mine," he states plainly, refusing to take the fall.

He's not the hero, or even the tragic hero. He never was. I'd been trying to force him into a role he was never meant to inhabit. He was miscast all along.

Mom nods. "Thought so." She glares at me. "So I assume this means you also took the money that disappeared from your father's bank account? The money he *swore* you couldn't possibly have taken?"

Out of the corner of my eye I see my Dad turn his face toward the window. He blinks. "Cloudy," I think he murmurs softly.

I am the worst daughter in the world.

The following afternoon passes like molasses as I wait to learn my fate—Putz has scheduled a follow-up meeting to iron out the details of my suspension.

I'm surprised when my father is the first to speak. His tone is so somber and steady that I barely recognize it. "Don't you think that the proximity of this rumor to the publication of Hannah's *Newsweek* article is a little suspicious?"

"I see no connection," Putz replies coolly. "As for Hannah's suspension, we—"

"I'd like to know more about the sources of these allegations before we move any further," Dad responds.

"As I mentioned before, Mr. Friedman, I'm not at liberty to disclose our sources."

"But you *are* at liberty to ruin the academic career of a model student with trumped-up sexual allegations? With slanderous gossip from a bunch of hysterical, jealous little girls?"

Putz squinches up his eyebrows. "Sir, even an esteemed *faculty member* has come forward to verify that your daughter was—"

"Are you familiar with Arthur Miller's *The Crucible*?"

Putz nods. "Of course." He seems pleased with himself for the first time all afternoon. "It's on the required summer reading list."

Dad reaches into his coat pocket and slams a copy of the play down on the desk with a resounding BOOM. "You. Have accused my daughter. Of dancing with the devil."

Putz swallows hard. He has no reply.

The allegations disappear as quickly as they arrived. Putz doesn't speak a single word to me for the rest of the year. I cannot help but feel betrayed by the place that has been my home these last four years. The place I've worked so hard to belong to. The place I thought would make me perfect. After all of the hair straightening and the paper writing and the presidential campaigns, all it took was one instance of me really speaking my mind for Danforth to turn its back on me completely. I realize that while four years ago I was "Danforth material," Danforth is no longer Hannah material.

My invisible camera and I watch as high school shrinks away in the rearview mirror, along with every lingering notion of valiant white knights and damsels in distress, of magical makeovers and popularity panaceas and transformations that start from without. It's a damn shame. I guess even when you try your hardest, real life doesn't work like Cinderella's. Although Rosewood will always look like something out of a fairy tale, I'm through with looking for the fairy tale. I want to start looking for me—the real me, not the me everyone else wants me to be. Things are going to be different from now on. And as our remaining days at Danforth melt inevitably away, I congratulate myself on this, my second official, decidedly adult decision.

Julian and I end whatever stormy relationship we had, and I throw out the razor from the back-zippered compartment of my wallet. I repay my dad for all the money I withdrew. Mac and I finish out our tenure on student government by passing a proposal that will help to override Putz's vetoes in the future. In the meantime, the Great Eight busies itself with plans for upcoming graduation parties to which I am not invited.

For as long as anyone can remember, Danforth graduation has taken place on the grand stone steps overlooking Rosewood. The boys wear blue blazers and regulation ties bearing the Danforth crest, and the girls wear preapproved white dresses—not eggshell or ivory or cream. Putz doesn't even let me take my dress out of the garment bag before checking it off the "approved attire" list in silence.

In years past, pairs of seniors made their way down the grand stone steps with their heads held high, waiting for their names to be called, waiting to claim their official Danforth diplomas. The dogwood blossoms were always in full bloom, decorative ice sculptures adorned Rosewood hill, and brass instruments playing the graduation march gleamed golden in the afternoon sun. But this year, it rains. We get our diplomas in the gym, we pose for some pictures, and high school is over.

chapter seventeen

EPILOGUES SUCK

"Can I play you something downstairs, honey bunny?"

"Sure, Dad."

I follow him into his recording studio, past the boxes of bicycle horns and lasers and monkey insulin syringes, past the Scrabble board and the old jazz charts, and I listen. Six freshly recorded tracks for the new album. Dad closes his eyes and taps his foot along with the songs while they play, stopping every now and then to scribble notes on the scores, which are spread out over every available surface. When I've heard everything, he turns to me nervously. Expectantly. "What do you think?"

"They're great, Dad."

They are. Some of them are hilariously witty, jam-packed with puns and raunchy klezmer clarinet solos. Others are deeply moving, simple and sincere. Each one of them really is a work of art. I realize that I can never be angry with my father for turning down a job at IBM.

My mother is beautiful. We look completely different.

Sam looks a lot like her, but they're nothing alike. He doesn't worry about what's going to happen ten seconds from now, let alone in ten years. Over the summer my brother and I reminisce about the Shoe Car and hang out in the tree house, and he teaches me about jazz soloing when we jam together in the basement. I don't know if he forgives me for all the times I shouted at him to stop playing the stupid piano so loud, for tattling, for pinching him too hard when we were kids. But I do know that I want to make it up to him.

I've finally discovered a friend who understands exactly what it's like to have a monkey for an older sister. Just in time for college. I never thought I'd miss my smelly little brother, but after this summer, I know that leaving him at home when I move to Connecticut is probably going to suck.

I am not going to miss the monkey. She's already sabotaged my packing process with strategic poops placed right in front of my dresser and my bookshelf and the washing machine. The first two were squishy and forced me to hop down the hall to the bathroom on one leg to wash my foot in the sink, but the last one was older—dried, and a little spiky—and now I'm finishing up my college packing with a bit of a limp.

"Hannah, you can't actually believe she left it there to harden on purpose," Mom laughs.

"I do, and she did," I say, loading another suitcase into the car.

"She loves you, you know."

"I don't love her back."

Before we leave, Mom runs me through her most rigorous

packing checklist ever. "Did you remember your flashlight? Antiseptic? Bottled water? Journal? Jeans? Do you have your Chinese juggling yo-yo? Your sewing kit? Saxophone? Hair straightener? Jeans? Did you remember your guitar? Your driver's license? Subway map? *Kotex?*" Suddenly my mother hugs me close to her. "Well, did you?"

"I remember, Mom," I tell her, returning the anomalous embrace. "How could I forget?"

Dear Universe,

As you are probably aware, I am starting a new school tomorrow. I still can't believe high school's really over. All I can say is thank goodness sometimes everything ends. I guess I owe you some thanks as well. I didn't really think you could wave a magic wand and just make things happen, but they happened anyway. And I don't want you to tell me to be careful what I wish for, because I'm not sorry that they did. I found friends and fell in love and I learned how to trust my own voice. I could have done with a few less boring classes and epic back stabbings, but I guess that was probably part of the plan, too.

I was hoping you might consider giving me a few tips as I move forward, given that we struck a pretty good deal the last time around. I promise to work hard, as always. I promise to appreciate what I've got. And I promise that if you show me how to figure these three things out, I'll make sure to spread the word however I can:

1. I want to find people who make my mind dance a polka. People who inspire me and encourage me and challenge me and who make me laugh until I cry.

2. I want to find out what I'm capable of. Not in student government, or in math class, or at the gym, or in the Great Eight. I want to find out what I'm capable of creating when the only person I'm doing it for is myself. And I want to love myself. I know that sounds really cheesy. But I also know that if I want to create something amazing, I can't pour so much time and energy into hating my calves. They're really not such bad calves, anyway. They always get me where I need to go. And besides, none of the biographies of great leaders or thinkers or artists ever end with, "and their contribution to the world would have been great indeed, if only they hadn't had such icky, icky calves."

3. I want to be myself, and I want to find out what the hell that means. I'll do whatever it takes.

Thank you in advance.

Yours wishfully,
Hannah Friedman

It's nighttime. I'm walking to my first college class, past the gorgeous Gothic stained glass tower of Sterling Memorial Library, when suddenly I'm surrounded by a sea of stars. All around me on the quad, small specks of light flash softly in the night before disappearing again into darkness. I reach out to cup a firefly in my hand—I don't even wait for it to glow—when someone stops me.

"Hey, don't I know you?" a dark-haired girl in a polo asks, studying me, trying to place my face.

"I don't think so," I tell her.

"Sorry, maybe not," she says after a moment, disappointed. "I guess I'm just so anxious to settle in here my mind is playing tricks on me." She starts to walk away. "Ohmigod!" she shouts suddenly, turning back. "I've got it! I think maybe we went to kindergarten together. Aren't you . . . That Monkey Girl?"

I'm so surprised that I accidentally squish the firefly in my hand. I look at my glowing palm and then look back at the girl, and I can't help but smile as I nod and admit that, "I am."

ACKNOWLEDGMENTS

I would like to thank all of the brilliant, passionate, and talented teachers who have inspired and encouraged me over the course of my education. Without you, I never would have discovered a love of language, faith in my own voice, or the guts to take on this project. You have inspired me to dig deeper and look closer, to never stop challenging myself, and to celebrate the absurdity and beauty all around us. Thanks especially to Caroline, Deb, Daniel, Laurie, Chris, Sarah, Skeff, Polina, and David. Teachers have the power to change the world, and you have changed mine in strange and wonderful ways.

The things that Ned, George, I., Jon, Jeremy, Brian, and Myles know about me collectively could probably fill seven much more humiliating books. Thank you all for making me laugh and listening to me whine and calling me out on my bullshit. Thank you for reading through drafts, giving me pep talks, and thank you in advance for letting me crash on your couches in case this whole "writer" thing doesn't work out.

You've all been terrible influences on me, and I wouldn't have it any other way.

I will be forever grateful to my magnificent editor Michele Matrisciani, to Carol Rosenberg, Larissa Henoch, Kim Weiss, Tom Sand, Peter Vegso, and to the entire team at HCI for their dedication to this book, for their enthusiasm, and for entrusting me with this amazing opportunity.

Mr. Thesaurus . . . I'm sure not being able to alter this drives you nuts, as I'm about to make several flagrant grammatical errors a restaurant accountant circle. Thank you for your patience! Thank you for skee ball and mambos and sundayloxloxlox. Thank you for believing in me and in this project and in home; endless cows!?!? Oh my, yes. The endlessest.

I would not be here without the support of my family. You have always believed in me, and I cannot think of a more profound gift. Except maybe if you let me borrow the car this weekend. . . .

Mom and Dad, I love you. Dorian and Racelle, you have kept me sane. Bub and Gramps, thank you for everything. Sam and Amelia, you are my favorite person and monkey (respectively) in the whole wide world. (And vice versa.)

POSTSCRIPT:
WRITING SUCKS

Writing is a wonderfully rewarding craft through which you can express your passions, learn about yourself, connect with others, and make some sense of this crazy world around us through the time-honored and universal tradition of the story. Writing is also a huge pain in the ass. Don't let anybody tell you otherwise.

Whenever I watch top athletes on the court, or star singers on the stage, I am always struck by the seeming effortlessness of their performances. For a long time, I was convinced that my favorite pieces of literature must have been the result of similarly seamless, elegant performances. My writing process is about as elegant as a frog in an old sock. I used to take this to mean that I sucked at writing, and possibly at life in general.

I was relieved when I began to research some of my favorite writers, only to discover that they were plagued by many of the same anxieties, frustrations, and doubts that I suffer from. The smithy of the soul can be a nasty, dirty, dangerous place. So if you love to play trombone but have a terrible time getting yourself to practice, if sewing necktie skirts gets you giddy but you're always putting off projects, if you dream of doing photography but can't drag yourself into a darkroom—you are not alone. You are not alone in confronting the torturous, uphill, 110°-in-the-shade, besieged-by-wasps-and-rabid-wolverines-and hailing-golf-ball-sized-blobs-of-snot creative process.

There are many excellent essays on the craft of writing. This is not one of those essays. Nor is this a poignant attempt to illustrate the ways in which writing has informed my mortal journey. Writing is a process, and I am still very much its pupil. If you are a professional author, or the ghost of Dickens past, please disregard everything I am about to say, because what the hell do I know? But if you, like me, always wonder how the heck stuff gets finished, here are a few things I learned while writing this book that I hope might be of use to you in your own artistic endeavors.

1. You cannot wait until whimsy beckons, because whimsy is a fickle muse.

The key to writing is to write. Make a schedule and set aside some time each day. No page limits, no word counts. Just set a timer, and keep your fingers moving for exactly that amount of time. On most days you'll have no idea where to start. But here's the fun part: every single one of my favorite passages in this book came after at least ten minutes of noodling around. I'd write my name. My address. I'd write, "I have nothing to write." And by and by, my mind would quiet and my fingers would take over and I'd emerge twenty minutes later with a few sentences that I didn't think totally sucked. Sentences that excited and surprised me. If I had waited until I "knew" exactly what I was going to do, nothing exciting or surprising would have been written. In fact, nothing would have been written at all.

2. Get used to the nine-tenths rule.

Nine-tenths of what you write is going to be, according to you, total crap. You have to wade through a lot of this supposed crap before you figure out what you're really trying to say. You're going to have to work and whittle and move things around before everything fits together. You may feel like you're on the wrong path. More likely, you'll feel like you're not even on a path at all, but rather, stranded in the inky blackness of an uncharted jungle labyrinth filled with people-eating plants and monkey poop. And you will hate all of your stupid ideas and want to give up, and maybe go watch TV and eat cookies. Don't do it. The reason that you're having a hard time finishing is the very same reason that you'll be able to finish. Having high standards for yourself makes it painful to muck through nine awful sentences before you get to a good one, but those same high standards will let you know when you finally do. So stop worrying about whether or not your project will be good, and focus on giving yourself permission to get to the good parts.

3. Work from a treasure map, not a blueprint.

I used to think Chapter One had to be perfect before I could move on to Chapter Two. I wanted to check it off of my little anal-retentive checklist. But that's not how creative projects work. They evolve from multiple angles at different speeds. Sometimes your very first sentence or lyric or brushstroke will be influenced by your very last, and you won't know how it all ties together until you get to the end.

I used to be Ms. Thesaurus, and I'd sit and stare at my computer for half an hour making sure I had the perfect word. This will kill your creative spirit and wear you down. In writing this book, I learned to appreciate the beauty of leaving things loose. If I need a word or a phrase or even an entire paragraph that I just can't seem to come up with, I'll leave myself a note and move on. You can always come back later. That's what editing is for. When you stop fixating on what your project should be, you get to discover what it is. And those two things are never the same. Your creative ideal is just a signpost indicating the direction in which you'll begin to search. Once you start to think about writing as the search for Tut's tomb instead of the laborious construction of a pyramid, you'll get more done and hate yourself a lot less. I promise.

4. Don't start poking holes in your cake before it's even in the oven.

I have never come up with a great idea banging my head against a wall, willing myself to produce one. It just doesn't work that way. In terms of raw creativity, your subconscious is valedictorian and your conscious mind is a drooling, earwax-eating dropout. Leave her out of this. When I was really "in the zone" while writing this book, it felt very much like a dream. The ideas came flowing out from somewhere deep within, and the hypercritical voice inside my head only served to disrupt that creative flow.

Then I made my Sucks Jar, a repurposed sugar bowl with a little slot for a spoon. Whenever my conscious mind starts to tell me "that's not funny," "that's not relevant," or "that just plain sucks," I write it down on a piece of paper and slip it in the jar. Then it's out of my head and I don't have to think about it anymore. When I look back at the notes now, I realize that if an editor or a friend were to tell me a fraction of those things, I would never let them read my stuff again. But we're all our own worst critics, and we can't get away from ourselves. That's why it's so important to delineate between pure creative time and hardcore "editing" time. If you give yourself the space to play out all of your wackiest ideas, a judgment-free zone to experiment and explore, you will surprise yourself. Then you can invite your inner critic back to the party to clean things up. If you let her in too early, she'll call in a noise complaint before you've even begun to boogie.

My best advice, for whatever that's worth, is to boogie on. Boogie on through self-doubt and boogie on through writer's block. Boogie on through as many drafts as it takes before you really feel your own creative beat. Soak up as much as you can from as many different artists as you can. Collect your confusions and heartbreaks. Record the rhythms of joyous moments and awkward pauses, and boogie along all the while.

Here's what I learned from this project: I do not always like writing, but I really like having written. And if someone with as many bad procrastinatory habits and nagging self-doubts as me can finish something, then you can too. Whether your creative outlet is painting or yodeling or carving canoes, have faith and have patience. If you really give yourself over to the rhythm of the process, if you shut up your inner critic for long enough to get into the groove, if you give yourself the gift of letting go and getting real messy before you get clean, then maybe you'll have just as much fun creating as you do in having created. Don't give up.

Love & Boogie-woogie,

Hannah Friedman

ABOUT THE AUTHOR

Hannah Friedman is neither avid trapeze artist nor professional philologist. Hannah Friedman cannot talk with turtles or bend spoons with her mind. Hannah has a regular amount of toes, enjoys thick cappuccino foam, and is allergic to cat dander. She grew up in New York, graduated from Yale, and promptly took a nap.

Hannah Friedman detests pretension, and therefore experiences no greater pleasure than writing all about herself in the third person. She also despises flagrant self-promotion, and encourages you to check out her TV shows, blogs, plays, and award-winning comedy songs at www.hannah friedman.com and www.youtube.com/writinghannah.

Hannah Friedman encourages you to follow your dreams. She aspires to save the world, or at least to invent a puppy-sized elephant.